CHORDS FOR
Jazz Gui[tar]

by Charlton Johnson

Also by Charlton Johnson:
Swing & Big Band Guitar (HL00695147)

ISBN 0-634-04714-0

HAL•LEONARD®
CORPORATION
7777 W. BLUEMOUND RD. P.O. BOX 13819 MILWAUKEE, WI 53213

In Australia Contact:
Hal Leonard Australia Pty. Ltd.
22 Taunton Drive P.O. Box 5130
Cheltenham East, 3192 Victoria, Australia
Email: ausadmin@halleonard.com

Visit Hal Leonard Online at
www.halleonard.com

About the Author

Charlton C. Johnson—A Biographical Sketch

Like most musicians growing up in Memphis, Tennessee, Charlton was exposed to a variety of musical styles including jazz, blues, and rhythm and blues. This eventually led Charlton to performances with a somewhat diverse roster of artists including The Count Basie Orchestra, Nancy Wilson, Joe Williams, Dianne Schuur, Dizzy Gillespie, Billy Eckstine, Max Roach, Lionel Hampton, James Moody, Ella Fitzgerald, George Benson, Albert King, James Cotton, Clarence "Gatemouth" Brown, Rufus Thomas, Carla Thomas, Phineas Newborn Jr., Calvin Newborn, Herman Green, Donald Brown, and James Williams. At the time of this writing, Charlton is teaching jazz guitar at the University of Memphis and also touring with blues legend Bobby "Blue" Bland.

A Special Thanks

The author wishes to first thank Almighty God.
Many thanks go out to Mom, Dad, Bernie, Tony, and the rest of my family for all of their love and support. Thanks also to everyone at Hal Leonard Corporation, The University of Memphis, Gene Rush, Tim Goodwin, Dr. Jack Cooper, Gerard Harris, Zxlema Zenobia Smith, Marvell Thomas.

Many thanks to the U. of M. bunch: Chip Henderson, James Hunter, John Bass, Matt Tutor, Danny Sykes, Logan Hanna, Jason Barden, Derrick Brookshire, David Bowen, and Kerry Movasaugh. You guys may never know just how much I've learned from you!

Dedication

This book is dedicated to all the musicians and teachers that have encouraged, entertained, and enlightened me over the years.

Preface

The idea for this book came from observing some of my students and noticing gaps in their chord voicing knowledge. They might play some chords that could be considered "advanced," but then not play an entire chord progression in an advanced and logical manner with good voice leading. In some cases they did not know the function of the notes in the voicings that they use, and as such rely simply on the "shapes." Along with the gaps, I've also noticed that some students don't know how or when to use certain chords.

Of course a thorough knowledge of chords and progressions is essential for jazz guitar. It is my contention that by studying basic voicings based on the low E, A, and D strings, the student will gain a foundation for any kind of chordal work that he or she may engage in. These chords are the foundation for comping, chord melody, and chord solos. They also can be used in medium and up tempo swing as well as ballads, blues, and Latin tunes.

While this book doesn't "invent" anything, it attempts to organize and present a systematic approach to the study of these basic chords. It attempts to give students a strong foundation upon which to build for future study. Unlike other books that merely diagram and catalog chords, this book requires the student to play exercises that take the chords all over the fretboard, which also improves fretboard knowledge in general. This book also contains exercises that illustrate the use of these chords in actual chord progressions, so that the student's harmonic awareness is improved.

The book is organized as follows:

Part I: The Voicings: Here the voicings are diagramed with fingerings and organized by string and top note. (At the University of Memphis, where I teach, I additionally ask students to write in the chord tone function for each diagram, i.e. 3rd, 5th, 7th, 9th etc.)

Part II: The Chord Exercises: These are the exercises for the various chords, arranged by family. The families are major, minor, min7b5, dominant, altered dominant, and diminished. These exercises go through all keys. At the end of the sections there are chord melody/solo exercises using the chords from that section. The first three sections have additional comping exercises.

Part III: Chord Progression Studies: This section puts the chords together in II–V7, minor II–V7, I–VI–II–V7, and diminished chord progressions. These exercises also go through all keys.

Part IV: Puttin' It All Together: It's time to do some comping, chord melody, and chord soloing examples using what we've studied in this book. This section begins with three stylistic comping examples based on a few popular jazz standards. Next, we have three simple melody examples from familiar tunes that are used to demonstrate chord melody playing. Finally, this section concludes with some improvised chord solos. These solos are over yet another group of chord progressions based on popular jazz standards.

Appendix I: Triads: An often overlooked chordal tool is the triad. This section diagrams some of the major, minor, augmented, and diminished triads that weren't covered earlier in the book.

Appendix II: Suggested Listening: Here, we have lists of musicians and recordings for you to check out. These lists are not comprehensive but can serve as a foundation for further chord study. Listening to the masters is extremely important for musical growth.

Again, in this book I'm attempting to give a strong foundation and background that will ultimately lead to sounding like a "jazz guitarist."

Contents

PART I
The Voicings

This section contains the fingering/chord tone diagrams for all of the chord voicings. The purpose here is twofold:

- Fingerings—While it is important to be systematic with fingerings, feel free to vary my suggested fingerings for your own use.
- Chord Tone Relationships—Studying these diagrams will help you learn the note functions of the voicings. Ideally you should be able to name the function of all notes (i.e. root , 3rd, 5th, etc.) for every voicing that you play.

CHORD ROOTS

The root of a chord can be defined in two simple ways:
- The note that the chord is built from based on the formula for a given chord type.
- The note from which the chord gets its name. For example, in the case of C7, the chord is built from the note C, where C is the root.

CONCEPT EXPLANATIONS

Some chord books list every chord with every possible root—i.e., Amaj7, Bmaj7, Cmaj7, etc. The Chord Reference/Fingering Library in this book lists chord diagrams without note names or keys. Since the roots of the chords are based on strings 6, 5, and 4, the desired chord is determined by the string and fret where the root is played.

RIGHT-HAND TECHNIQUE

Most of the chords in this book can be strummed with a flatpick. However, it is a good idea to also practice playing chords with the fingers (classical guitar style) or a combination of pick and fingers. With the pick and fingers technique, the pick plays the lowest note, while the fingers (2, 3, 4) play the remaining notes of the chord.

DIAGRAM/SYMBOL EXPLANATION

Each chord in the library is illustrated as seen below:

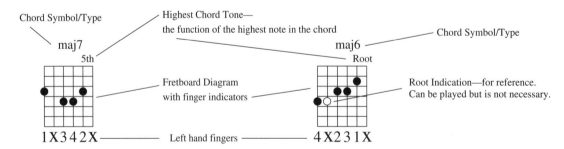

The roots of the chords will be based on strings 6, 5, and 4. This will be indicated at the top of each page in the Chord Reference/Fingering Library. Also observe that the voicings rarely use "doubled" notes. In general, each note in the chord will be a different note. A notable exception to this rule will come with some triad voicings.

NOTES ON THE GUITAR FRETBOARD

The chords that we're studying have roots on the lowest three strings, i.e., the low E, A, and D strings. Therefore, it may be helpful to take a look at the notes on these strings.

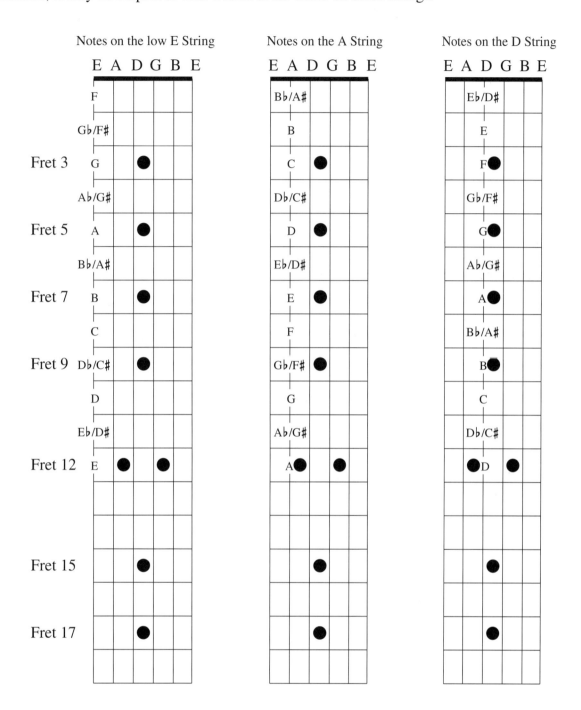

CHORD FAMILIES AND SUBSTITUTION

As stated earlier the chord diagrams are arranged by family. The term "chord family" refers to chords that share the same function in a chord progression. For example, Cmaj7 and C6/9 are both in the major chord family because they function the same way in a given chord progression. Therefore, Cmaj7 and C6/9 could be interchangeable in a given chord progression. This interchangeability is also called *substitution*. So, chords that are in a given family can very often substitute for each other in a given chord progression. This idea enables us to do a lot in our chord applications—namely, comping, chord melody, and chord soloing. The six chord families we'll study are major, minor, min7b5, dominant, altered dominant, and diminished.

OPEN AND CLOSED CHORD VOICINGS

In general, a *closed* voicing is one in which the notes are arranged in the closest possible configuration; i.e., no additional chord tones can go in between the notes in a closed voicing. This usually means that the intervals between notes are no larger than a 4th and are frequently as small as a minor 2nd. As a result, these voicings, while pretty to hear, can be difficult to finger on the guitar as can be seen in the second measure below.

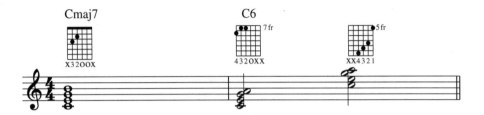

An *open* voicing is one in which the notes are spread out far enough that chord tones can be added between the notes of the voicing. Open voicings therefore require wide intervals of at least a 3rd and larger between chord tones. See examples below.

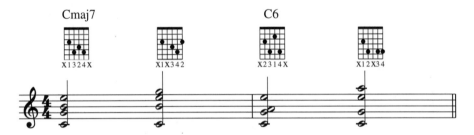

Open voicings generally sound larger and fuller because they cover a wider range than closed voicings. The guitar lends itself well to open voicings because the standard tuning is an open voicing of Em7(add11). See below.

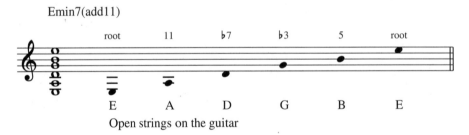

Open strings on the guitar

DOUBLING NOTES

As stated earlier, most of the chord voicings that we're studying will not have doubled or repeated notes. In other words, we want each note in a given chord to be different.

However, in the case of triads, we will look at voicings that have doubled notes because these voicings fatten up the sound of the triads. As you know, a triad by definition contains three notes. In the exercises that come later, we'll use four-note voicings, in which one of the triad notes is doubled and raised or lowered an octave.

Chord Reference/Fingering Library

MAJOR CHORD FAMILY

Root: 6th string—Triads: Closed, Open, w/ Doubles

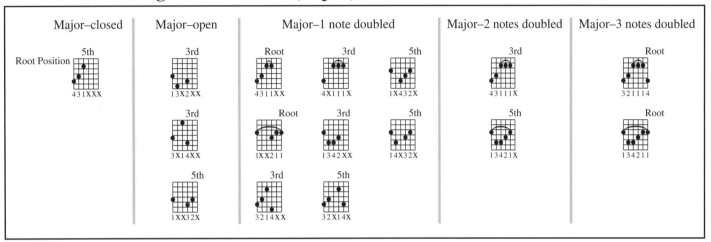

Root: 6th string—Sixth, Seventh, and Extended Chord Types

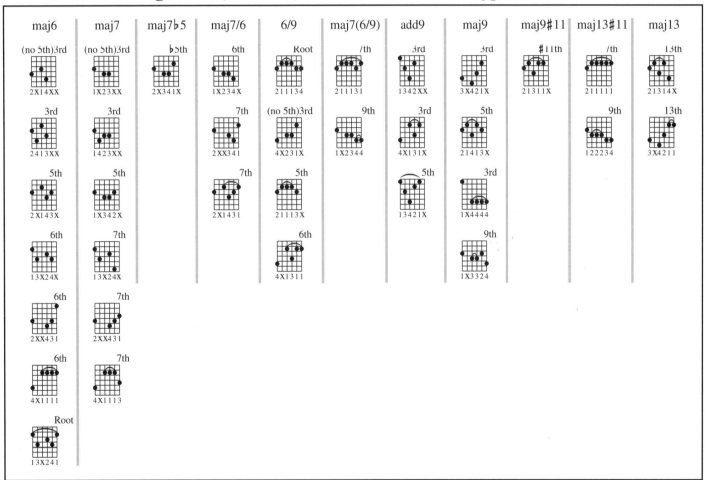

Substitution Notes:

While major type chords can generally substitute for each other, it is best to choose chord types that don't clash with the melody. Always listen! Majors that contain a 7th are often substituted for each other, i.e., maj7, maj7/6, maj7/(6/9), maj9, etc. Majors that contain a 6th and/or 9th, but no 7th are often substituted, i.e., 6, 6/9, add9. While majors that do not have a 7th are often substituted for majors with a 7th, the reverse won't always work. For example, a 6/9 used in place of a maj7 will work more often than a maj7 played in place of a 6/9.

Root: 5th string—Triads: Closed, Open, w/ Doubles

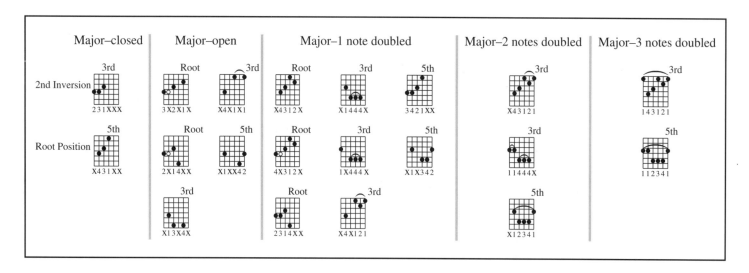

Root: 5th string—Sixth, Seventh, and Extended Chord Types

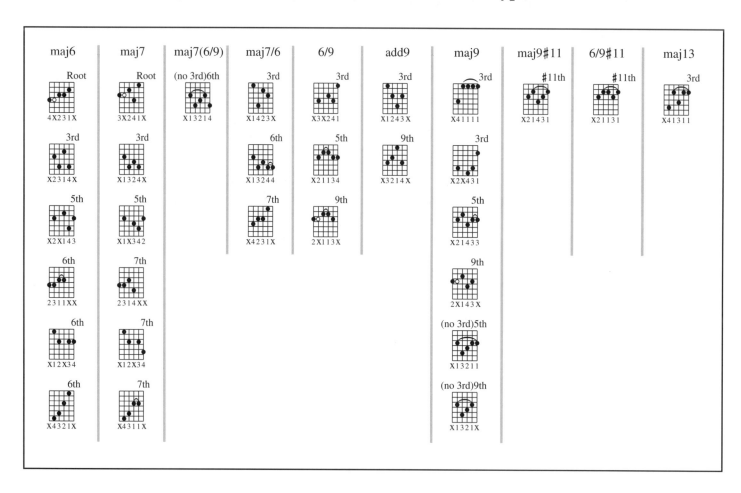

Root: 4th string—Triads: Closed, Open, w/ Doubles

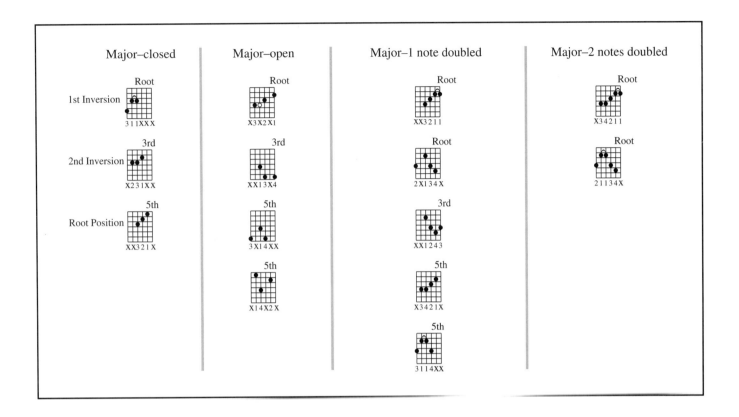

Root: 4th string—Sixth, Seventh, and Extended Chord Types

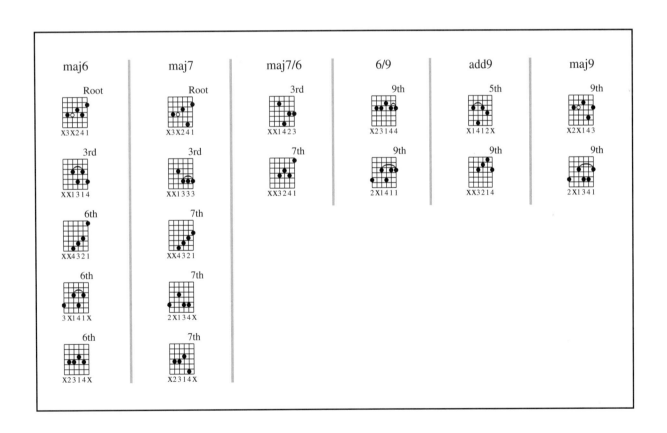

MINOR CHORD FAMILY

Root: 6th string—Triads: Closed, Open, w/ Doubles

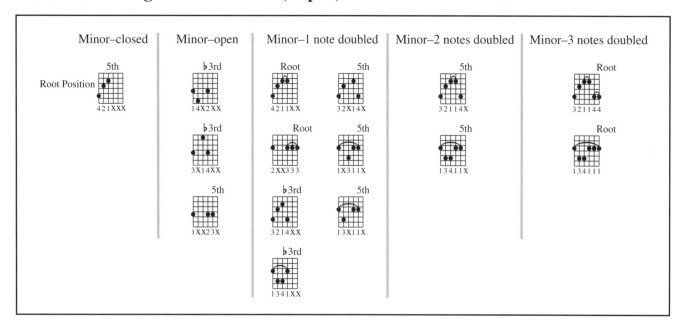

Root: 6th string—Sixth, Seventh, and Extended Chord Types

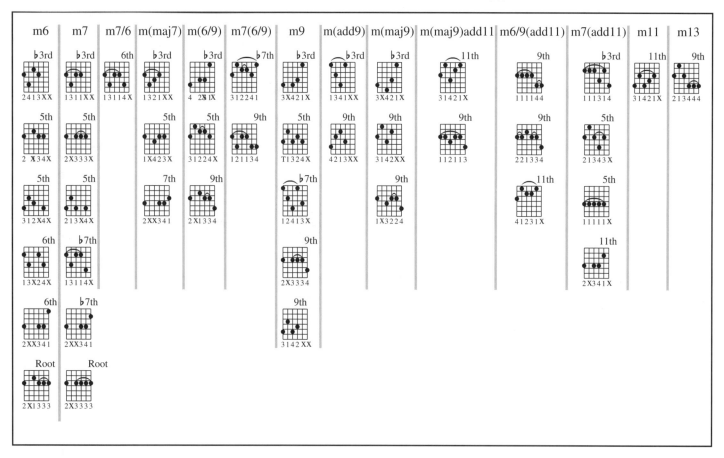

Substitution Notes:

While minor type chords can generally substitute for each other, it is best to choose chord types that don't clash with the melody. Minors that contain a ♭7th are often substituted for each other, i.e., m7, m9, m11, etc. Minors that contain a 6th and/or 9th, but no 7th are often substituted, i.e., m6, m6/9, m(add9). Minors that have a (major)7th are not usually substituted for minors with a ♭7th and vice versa.

Root: 5th string—Triads: Closed, Open, w/ Doubles

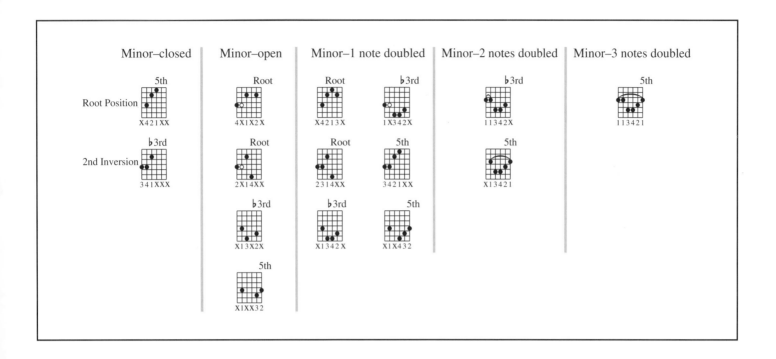

Root: 5th string—Sixth, Seventh, and Extended Chord Types

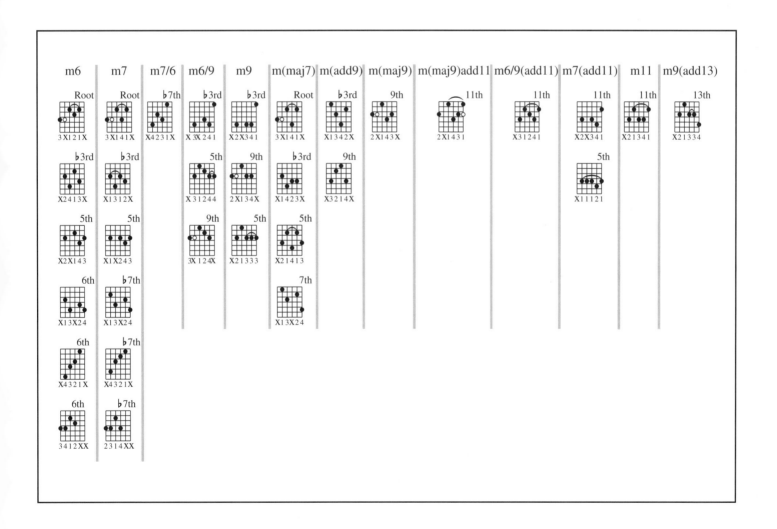

Root: 4th string—Triads: Closed, Open, w/ Doubles

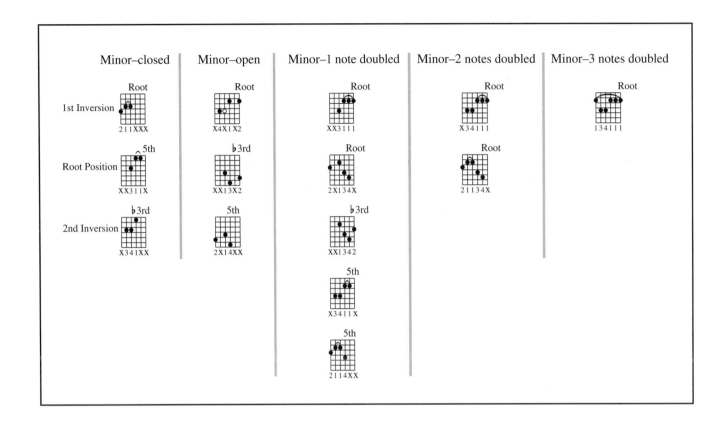

Root: 4th string—Sixth, Seventh, and Extended Chord Types

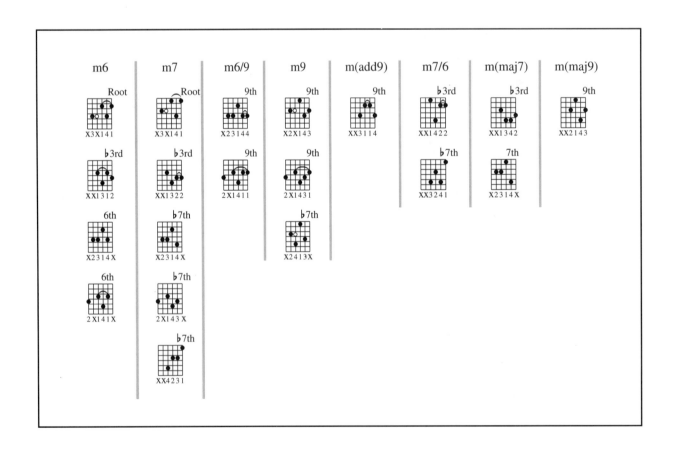

DOMINANT CHORD FAMILY

Root: 6th string—Seventh and Extended Chord Types

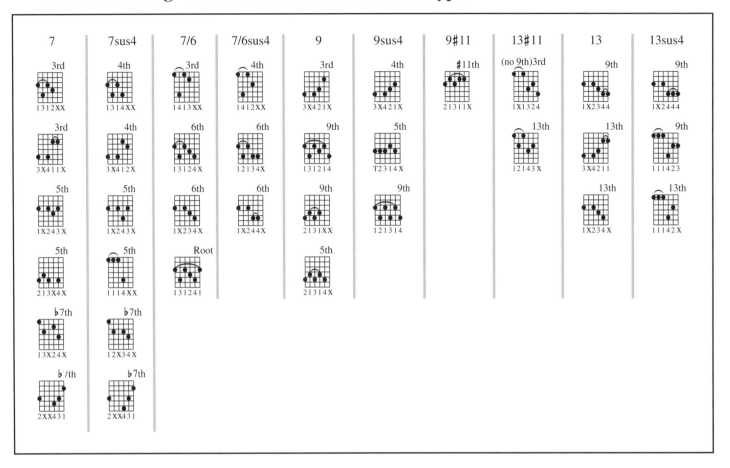

Root: 5th string—Seventh and Extended Chord Types

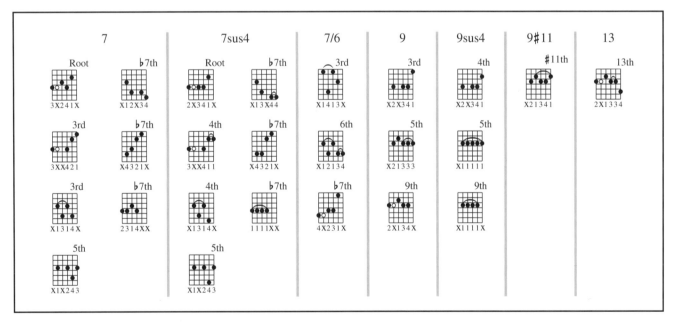

Substitution Notes:

While many dominant type chords can substitute for each other, it is best to choose chord types that don't clash with the melody. Always listen! Dominants that contain a 3rd are often substituted for each other, i.e., 7, 9, ♯11, 13, etc. Dominants with a 4th can usually be substituted, i.e., 7sus4, 7/6(sus4), 9sus4, etc. The 7/6 chord is usually a good substitution for a 13th.

Root: 4th string—Seventh and Extended Chord Types

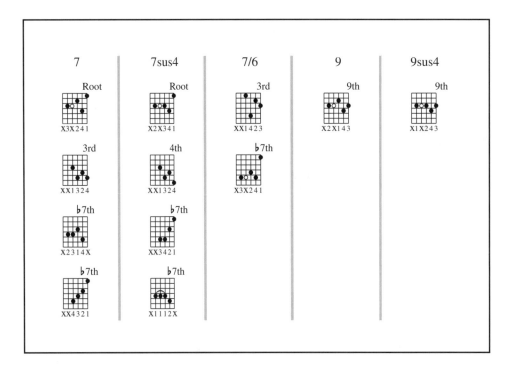

ALTERED DOMINANT CHORD FAMILY

Root: 6th string—Augmented Triads: Closed, Open, w/ Doubles

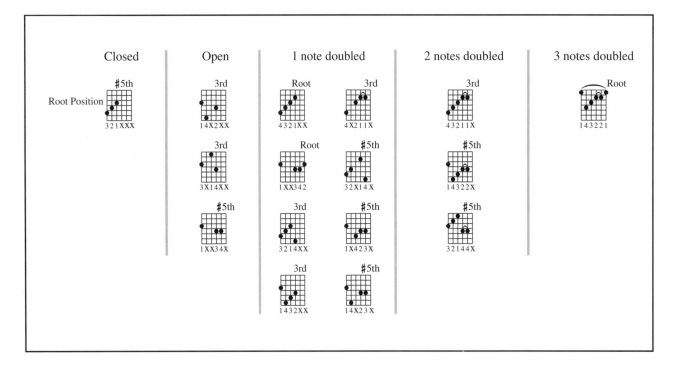

Substitution Notes:

While many altered dominant type chords can substitute for each other, it is best to choose chord types that don't clash with the melody. Altered dominant substitutions depend on how the 5th and the 9th are altered. Generally speaking, a chord with an altered 5th or 9th cannot be substituted for one with an unaltered 5th and/or 9th. Also, as most altered dominants resolve to another chord, try to find a voicing that leads to the next chord in a smooth and musical manner.

Root: 6th string—Seventh and Extended Chord Types

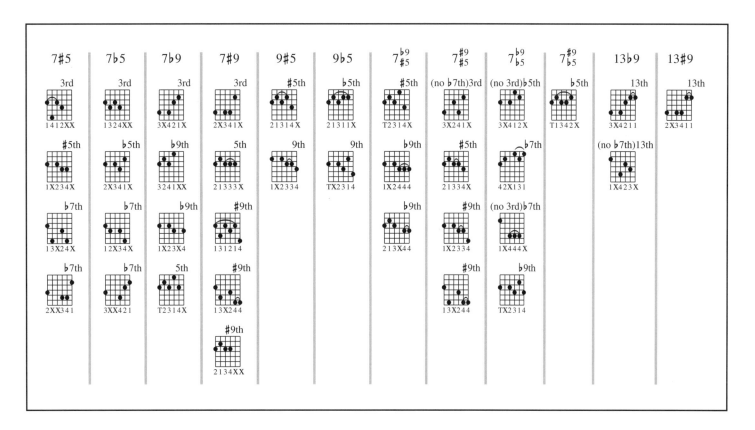

Root: 5th string—Augmented Triads: Closed, Open, w/ Doubles

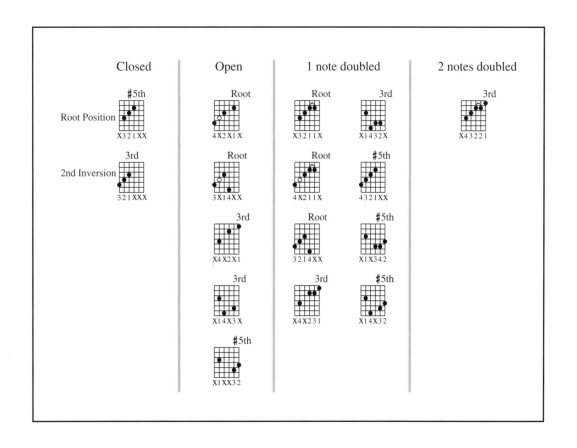

Root: 5th string—Seventh and Extended Chord Types

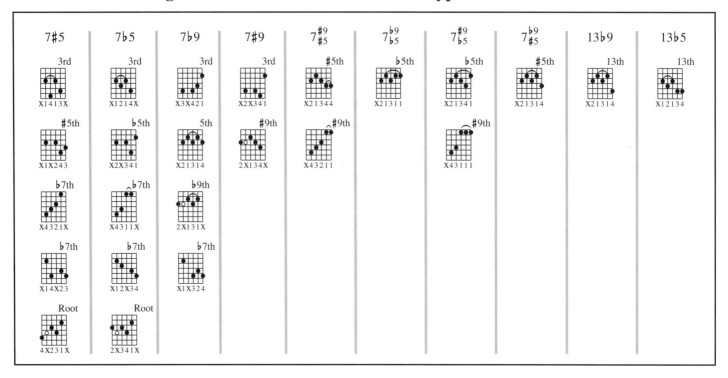

Root: 4th string—Augmented Triads: Closed, Open, w/ Doubles

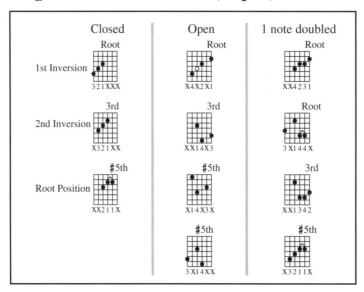

Root: 4th string—Seventh and Extended Chord Types

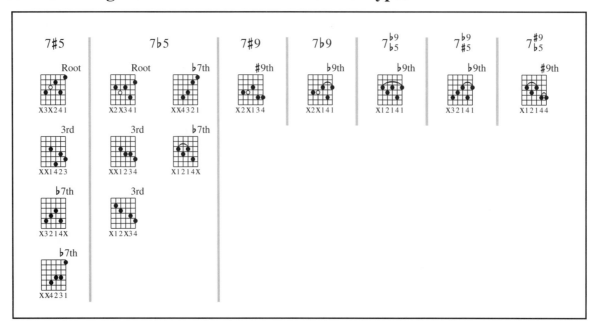

MINOR 7♭5 CHORD FAMILY

Root: 6th string—Seventh and Extended Chord Types

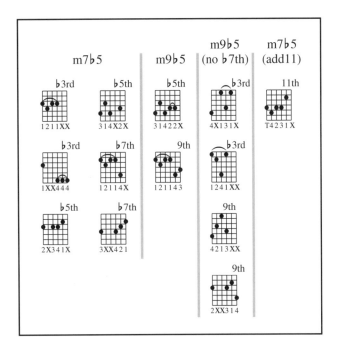

Root: 5th string—Seventh and Extended Chord Types

Root: 4th string—Seventh and Extended Chord Types

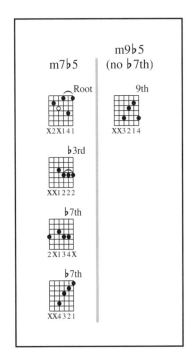

Substitution Notes:

While most m7♭5 type chords can substitute for each other, it is best to choose chord types that don't clash with the melody. Always listen!

DIMINISHED CHORD FAMILY

Root: 6th string—Diminished Triad, Diminished 7th

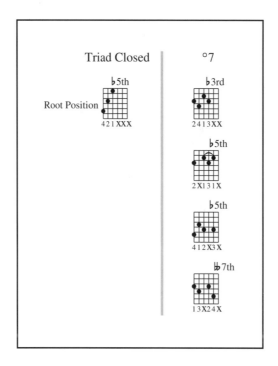

Root: 5th string—Diminished Triad, Diminished 7th

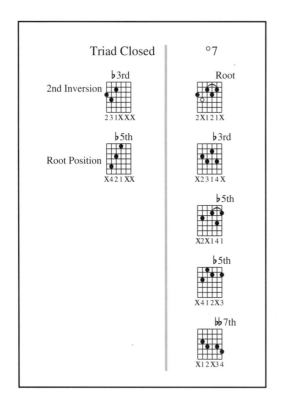

Root: 4th string—Diminished Triad, Diminished 7th

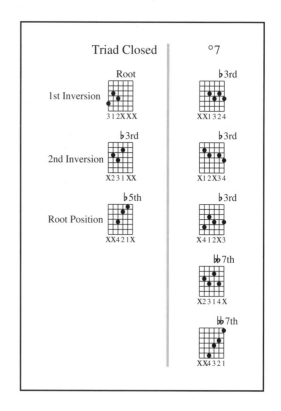

Substitution Notes:

While most diminished type chords can substitute for each other, it is best to choose chord types that don't clash with the melody. Always listen! The diminished triad is not used very often today but, it can be useful in chord melody playing.

PART II

The Chord Exercises

In this section, the exercises are grouped into various chord families in order to show relationships and substitution possibilities. The families are:

1. Major Type—Triads, Sixth, Seventh, and Extended Chords
2. Minor Type—Triads, Sixth, Seventh, and Extended Chords
3. Dominant Type—Seventh and Extended Chords
4. Altered Dominant Type—Seventh and Extended Chords
5. Minor 7♭5 Type—Seventh and Extended Chords
6. Diminished Type—Triads and Seventh Chords

Additionally, at the end of each section there are chord melody/solo and comping studies that utilize various chords in that particular section.

HOW THE CHORD EXERCISES WORK

A few explanations are necessary so that you can get the most out of the chord exercises.

In each exercise you will see chord diagrams and chord symbols with chord voicing indicator number(s) beneath them. The chord voicing indicator number indicates the chord voicing being used by referring to the string that the root is on along with the highest chord tone in the voicing. For example, if you see the symbol Cmaj7 with 6s-3rd under it, this means you are to play the voicing from The Chord Reference/Fingering Library that has the root on the sixth string and the 3rd of the chord (in this case the note E) as the highest note. See the examples below.

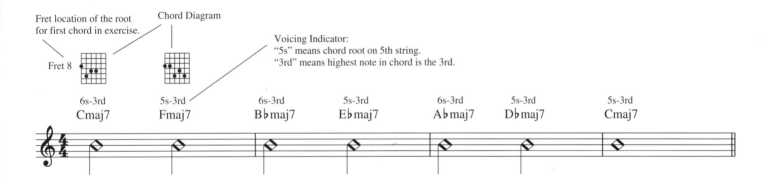

Occasionally there may be a need to indicate the string that the highest note is on. In those cases, the string is indicated as in the following example:

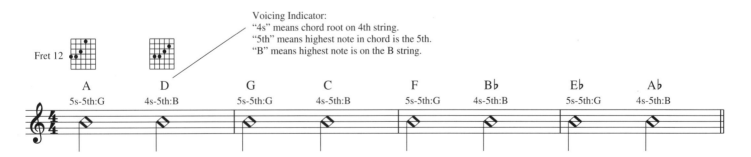

Major Chord Formula and Discussion

In order to construct the major chords, we have to follow the formulas for each chord. The formulas use the numbered major scale as seen below (key of C major):

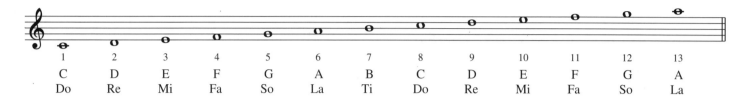

1	2	3	4	5	6	7	8	9	10	11	12	13
C	D	E	F	G	A	B	C	D	E	F	G	A
Do	Re	Mi	Fa	So	La	Ti	Do	Re	Mi	Fa	So	La

Or, referring to the chord tone chart:

Scale tone	Common name
1	Root or tonic
2	Second
3	Third
4	Fourth
5	Fifth
6	Sixth
7	Seventh
8	Octave
9	Ninth
10	Tenth, octave above Third
11	Eleventh, octave above Fourth
12	Twelfth, octave above Fifth (Not referred to often in jazz)
13	Thirteenth, octave above Sixth

The chord formulas are then constructed basically from "stacking thirds," i.e. using every other note of the scale. Study the table below:

Name	Formula	Notes in C	Chord symbol for C
Major Triad	root, 3rd, 5th	C, E, G	C
Major Sixth	root, 3rd, 5th, 6th	C, E, G, A	C6
Major Seventh	root, 3rd, 5th, 7th	C, E, G, B	Cmaj7
Major Ninth	root, 3rd, 5th, 7th, 9th	C, E, G, B, D	Cmaj9
Major add 9	root, 3rd, 5th, 9th	C, E, G, D	Cadd9
Major Sixth Nine	root, 3rd, 5th, 6th, 9th	C, E, G, A, D	C_9^6
Major Nine Sharp Eleven	root, 3rd, 5th, 7th, 9th, #11th	C, E, G, B, D, F#	Cmaj9#11
Major Thirteenth	root, 3rd, 5th, 7th, 9th, #11th, 13th	C, E, G, B, D, F#, A	Cmaj13

MAJOR TRIADS—ONE NOTE DOUBLED

Triads, by definition, contain only three different notes. These exercises use four-note voicings in which the fourth note is created by doubling one of the triad notes and either raising or lowering it an octave. This gives the triad a fuller sound.

MAJOR CHORDS—SEVENTH, SIXTH, AND EXTENDED

Approaching the Applications

Now we want to look at some concepts that will allow us to apply the chords we have learned to some example chord progressions. There are three areas that we want to look at:

- Chord Melody
- Chord Soloing
- Comping

CHORD MELODY

This term refers to playing a given melody in chords. We're going to look at three basic approaches:

- Chord Family Approach—The idea here is to play a chord from the given chord family on every note in the song's melody. We approach this by first studying scales and applying chords to each note of the scale.
- Chord Pair Approach—This approach generates chord scales by using two or more chords from different chord families and inverting them. With this approach, a chord is played on every note of the melody like it is with the Chord Family Approach discussed above.
- Alternating Chord/Note Style—For a given melody chords are placed only on beats 1 and 3. On beats 2 and 4 we play single notes. This can create the effect of self-accompaniment. Again, we develop this idea by first studying scales and applying chords from the given chord family only on beats 1 and 3.

Remember that the chords I'm using in the exercises are only suggestions to help you get started. Feel free to use other chords or voicings as you see fit. Experiment!

CHORD SOLOING

Just as we can play a given melody with chords, it is also possible to improvise melodies with chords underneath. This is an amazing skill that guitarists like Wes Montgomery, Joe Pass, and others have mastered. We will approach chord soloing from the perspective of scales. The basic idea is that if we learn a chord to play under each note in a scale, then we can improvise melodies with the chords. The "Chord Family Approach," the "Chord Pair Approach," and the "Alternating Chord/Note Style" apply here as they did in the chord melody discussion above. As such, chord melody and chord soloing will be studied in the same section. Again, remember that the chords I'm using in the exercises are only suggestions to help you get started. Feel free to use other chords or voicings as you see fit. Experiment!

COMPING

Comping comes from the word "accompaniment." This is a huge part of playing jazz guitar. As guitarists, we are asked to accompany singers, horn players, bassists, and others. To "comp" behind someone means to provide an atmosphere of chordal and rhythmic support for that person. There are also stylistic considerations, based on the song and the setting. All musical styles—swing, bossa nova, funk, rock, etc.—have characteristics that a good accompanist knows. We're going to look at three styles:

- Bossa Nova: Actually, we're going to look at two variations of a basic Bossa Nova rhythm.

    1) The first approach is to play each chord with the written rhythm.

    2) The second approach adds a bass line underneath the rhythm from the first approach.
- Swing: We're going to touch on two swing styles.

    1) The first style applies the "Killer Joe" rhythm to the example chord progression. "Killer Joe" is a Benny Gholson composition with a rhythmic figure that has been very influential to jazz musicians. This rhythm is actually a variation of the "Charleston" rhythm from the dance craze of the 1920s. Variations of the Charleston rhythm are very popular with jazz musicians.

2) The second swing style is the basic big band rhythm guitar style. In this style, the guitar plays three-note voicings derived from 7th chord voicings. These voicings are played "4 to the bar" or, more plainly, on every beat. This was the prevalent style for guitarists in the big band era. One of the most notable rhythm guitarists was Freddie Green of the Count Basie Orchestra.

- Jazz Ballad: This style calls for smooth, lush chords. The chords sustain in this style more than the others. The goal here is to bring out the beauty of the song by choosing thick, orchestral chord voicings.

VOICE LEADING

Of course we want all of our chords to sound as musical as possible. This is best accomplished through *voice leading*. While a full discussion on voice leading is beyond the scope of this book, I do want to give you a basic idea of what it is and how it applies to what we're doing. With voice leading, we follow the movement of the notes in a chord progression. Our goal is to choose voicings that allow the notes in each chord to travel the shortest distance to the next chord. We want the notes in a given chord to "lead" to the next chord smoothly, logically, and musically. See the example below.

Example Chord Progression

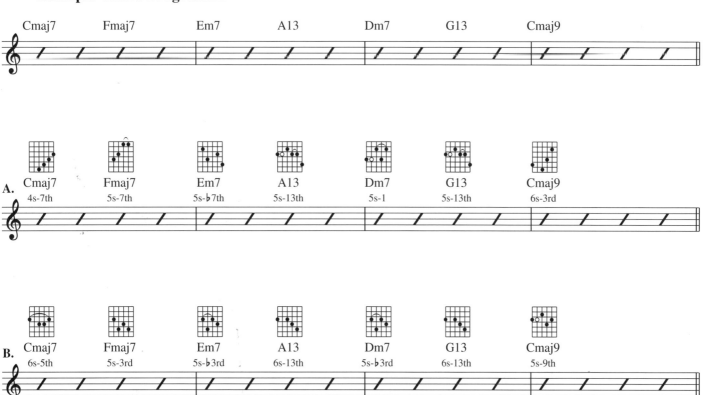

In the example above, we have a four-bar chord progression and two possible ways to voice the chords.

- Version A—This is bad voice leading because the notes in the voicings go all over the place, moving unnecessarily from chord to chord. The chords jump all over the neck with nothing tieing them together. As a result, the progression doesn't sound as smooth as it could.
- Version B—This is good voice leading because the notes in the voicings don't travel very far to get to the next chord. This version is both smooth and musical.

So, for any chord progression that you play, try to connect or transition the chords in a smooth and musical way. Pay attention to and critique the voice leading in the examples in this book. This is of particular importance in all of the application sections of this book.

Applications for Major

The goal is to be able to play a chord underneath each note of a given or improvised melody. Of course, the melodies must fit the chord progression of the song that we're playing. As stated earlier, we're going to look at scales that we can play using chords.

CHORD FAMILY APPROACH

One way to harmonize a scale is to put a chord from the chord family (major, minor, etc.) under each note of the scale. For example, if the given chord in a song is Cmaj7, we can play a C major scale in chords by placing various C major family chords (i.e. Cmaj6, Cmaj9, etc.) under each note in the C major scale. This will work for every note in the scale except the 4th degree. It won't work for the 4th degree because there is no common major type chord with a 4th or 11th. See below.

C Major Scale in Chord Family Style—Play through these chords a few times, then proceed to the exercises.

Chord Melody/Chord Solo Exercises for Chord Family Style—Play the appropriate chord for each note of the melodies below, based on the scale above.

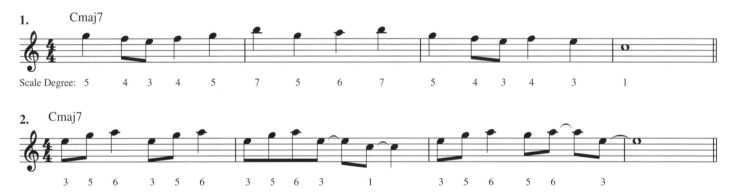

CHORD PAIR APPROACH

Another approach would be to use two (or more) chords from different chord families on various notes in the scale. For example, if the given chord is Cmaj7, we can play a C major scale in chords by dividing the scale into primary chord tones, and scale tones. We can then use the C major Chord Family on the primary chord tones, i.e., 1, 3, 5, and 7, and Dm7 on the other tones (scale tones or secondary tones), i.e., 2, 4, 6. The general rule for determining the 2nd chord of the chord pair is to use a chord based on either the next scale degree above or below the given chord. In this example, Cmaj7 is the primary chord and Dm7 is the secondary chord as it is the chord that is the next scale degree up from C. (See Part III: Chord Progression Studies.) Note that chords from other scale degrees can also be used with or without the secondary chord.

Generally, the Chord Pair approach sounds more colorful than the Chord Family approach. However, good chord solos, whether improvised or arranged, often use both approaches.

C Major Scale using Chord Pair Approach—Play through these chords a few times, then proceed to the exercises.

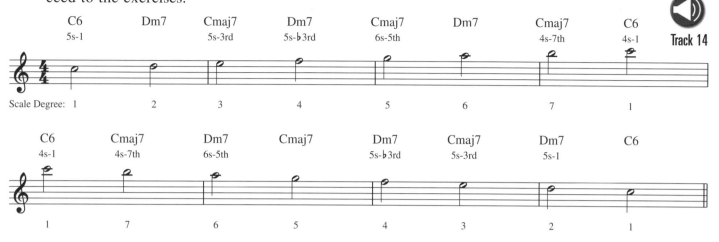

Chord Melody/Chord Solo Exercises for Chord Pair Approach—Play the appropriate chord for each note of the melodies below, based on the scale above.

ALTERNATING CHORD/NOTE STYLE

In this style the idea is to play a melodic line while simultaneously playing a chord on beats one and three of each bar. This style is based on the premise that in playing a single-note melodic line or melody, only one finger at a time is used for each note, therefore the other fingers can grab chords under some of the melody notes. Of course it is preferable for the melody notes to be the top notes of the chords. The chords used are from the given chord family. See below.

C Major Scale in Alternating Chord/Note Style—Play this a few times, then proceed to the exercises.

Track 15

Play the appropriate chord on note indicated (↓) only!

COMPING SECTION

Given the example chord progression below, we will apply different styles to it using chords studied thus far. Each comping style is indicated with the corresponding exercise.

Comping Study Progression

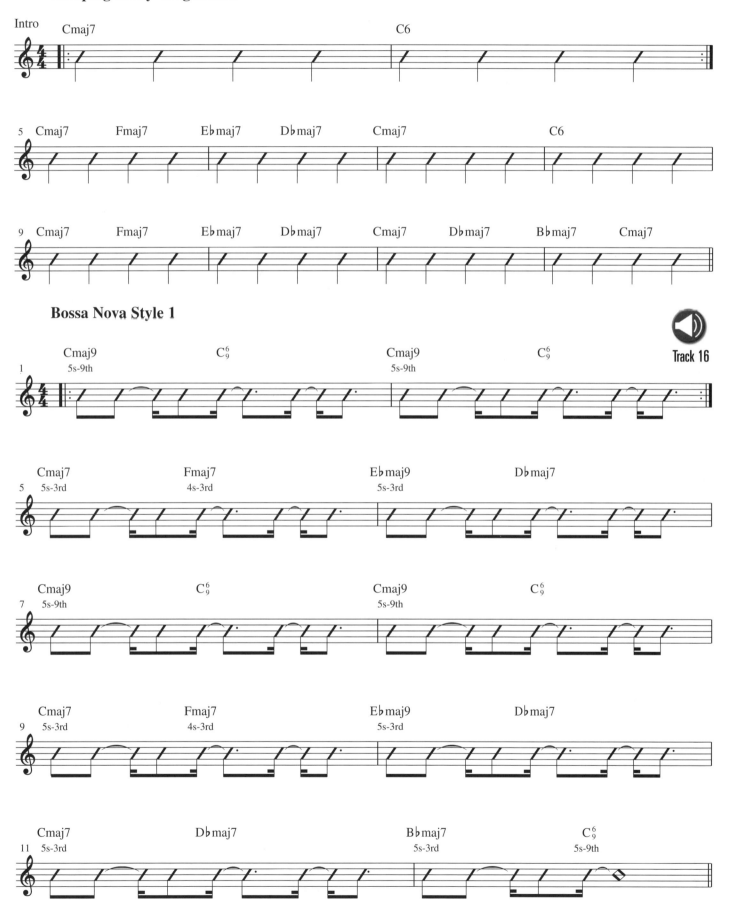

Bossa Nova Style 1

Track 16

Bossa Nova Style 2

This example is like the previous one except that a bass line has been added. Play the bass line with your thumb and the chords with fingers 1, 2, and 3 of the right hand. Optionally, a flatpick and fingers 2, 3, and 4 can also be used.

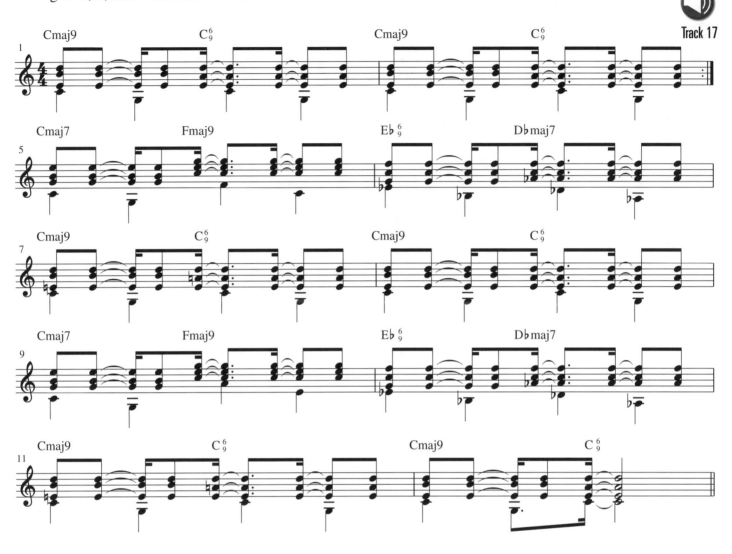

Track 17

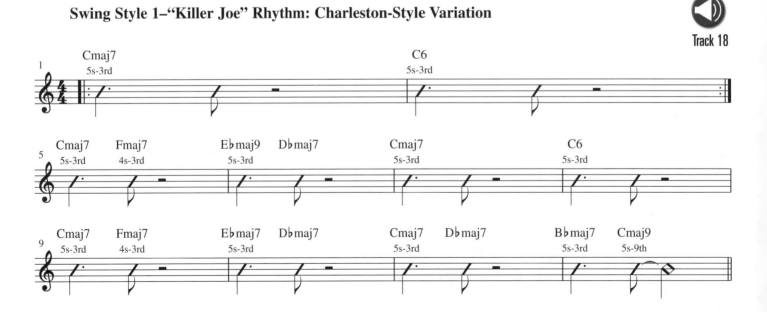

Swing Style 1–"Killer Joe" Rhythm: Charleston-Style Variation

Track 18

40

Swing Style 2–Four-to-the-Bar Style

In this style we play a chord on each beat of the measure. Also, we want to to play each chord without sounding the note on the B string. This is reminiscent of the Freddie Green style. Mr. Green played with the Count Basie Orchestra and was often called "Mr. Rhythm."

Ballad Style

The idea here is simply to play as "pretty" as possible!

Minor Chord Formula and Discussion

In order to construct the minor chords, we have to follow the formulas for each chord. The formulas use the numbered Dorian mode as seen below (mode of C Dorian):

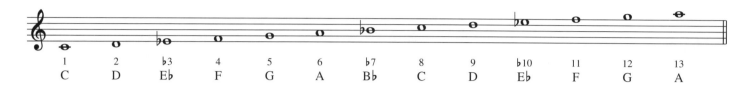

| 1 | 2 | ♭3 | 4 | 5 | 6 | ♭7 | 8 | 9 | ♭10 | 11 | 12 | 13 |
| C | D | E♭ | F | G | A | B♭ | C | D | E♭ | F | G | A |

Or, referring to the chord tone chart:

Scale tone	Common name
1	Root or tonic
2	Second
♭3	Flatted Third, or Minor Third
4	Fourth
5	Fifth
6	Sixth
♭7	Flatted Seventh
8	Octave
9	Ninth
♭10	Minor Tenth, octave above Minor Third
11	Eleventh, octave above Fourth
12	Twelfth, octave above Fifth (Not referred to often)
13	Thirteenth, octave above Sixth

The chord formulas are then constructed basically from "stacking thirds," i.e. using every other note of the scale. Study the table below:

Name	Formula	Notes in C	Chord symbol for C
Minor Triad	root, ♭3rd, 5th	C, E♭, G	Cm
Minor Sixth	root, ♭3rd, 5th, 6th	C, E♭, G, A	Cm6
Minor Seventh	root, ♭3rd, 5th, ♭7th	C, E♭, G, B♭	Cm7
Minor Ninth	root, ♭3rd, 5th, ♭7th, 9th	C, E♭, G, B♭, D	Cm9
Minor add 9	root, ♭3rd, 5th, 9th	C, E♭, G, D	Cm(add9)
Minor Sixth Nine	root, ♭3rd, 5th, 6th, 9th	C, E♭, G, A, D	Cm§
Minor Eleventh	root, ♭3rd, 5th, ♭7th, 9th, 11th	C, E♭, G, B♭, D, F	Cm11
Minor Thirteenth	root, ♭3rd, 5th, ♭7th, 9th, 11th, 13th	C, E♭, G, B♭, D, F, A	Cm13

MINOR TRIADS—ONE NOTE DOUBLED

Triads, by definition, contain only three different notes. These exercises use four-note voicings where the fourth note is created by doubling one of the triad notes and either raising or lowering it an octave. This gives the triad a fuller sound.

Track 21

Track 22

44

MINOR CHORDS—SEVENTH, SIXTH, AND EXTENDED

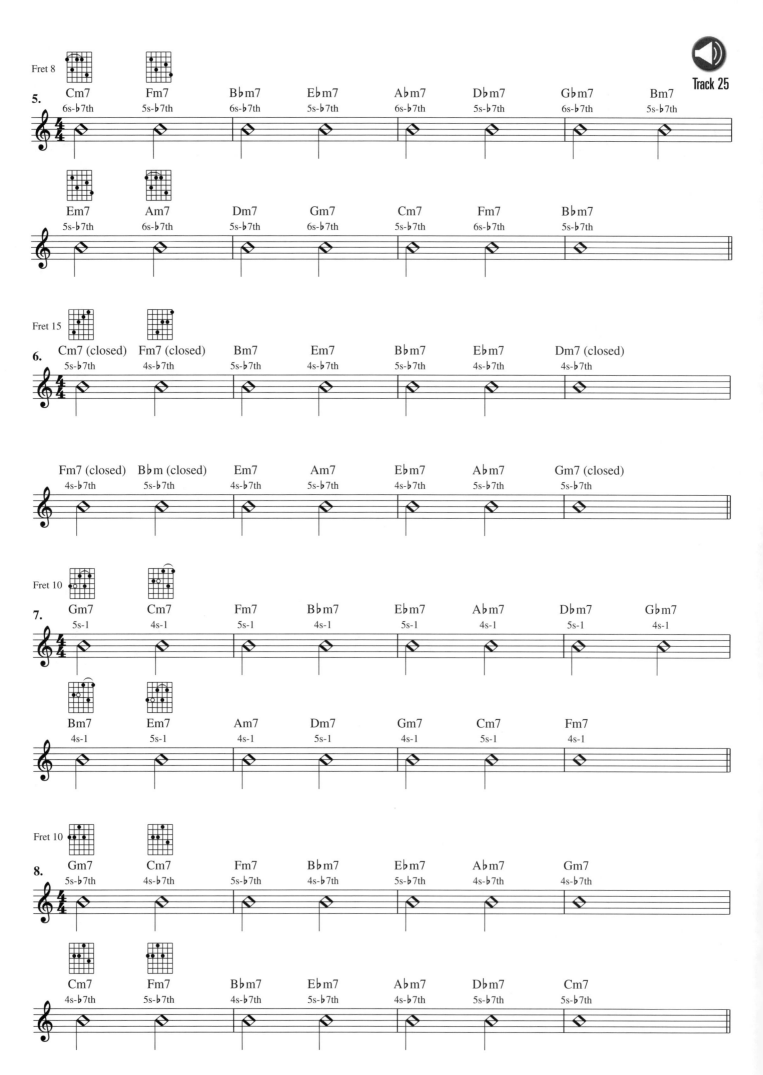

Applications for Minor

CHORD FAMILY APPROACH

C Minor Scale in Chord Family Approach—(Dorian Mode)

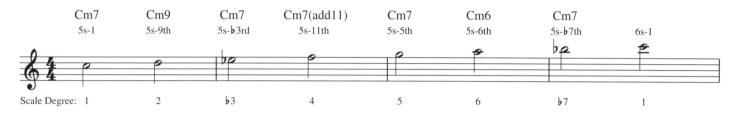

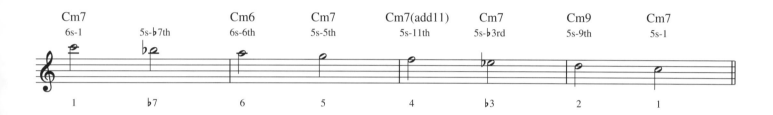

Chord Melody/Chord Solo Exercises for Chord Family Approach—Play the appropriate chord for each note of the melodies below, based on the scale above.

CHORD PAIR APPROACH

C Minor Scale using Chord Pair Approach—(Dorian Mode)

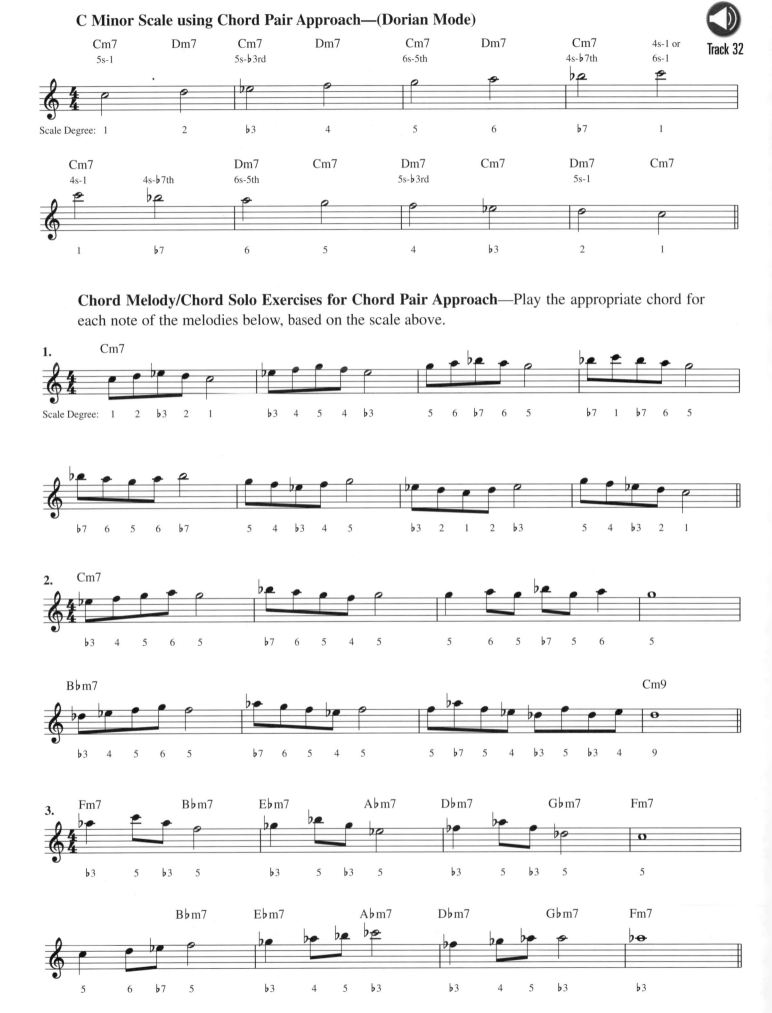

ALTERNATING CHORD/NOTE STYLE

C Dorian Mode in Alternating Chord/Note Style—Play this a few times, then proceed to the exercises.

Play appropriate chord on note indicated (↓) only!

COMPING SECTION

Given the example chord progression below, we will apply different styles to it using chords studied thus far. Each comping style is indicated with the corresponding exercise.

Comping Study Progression

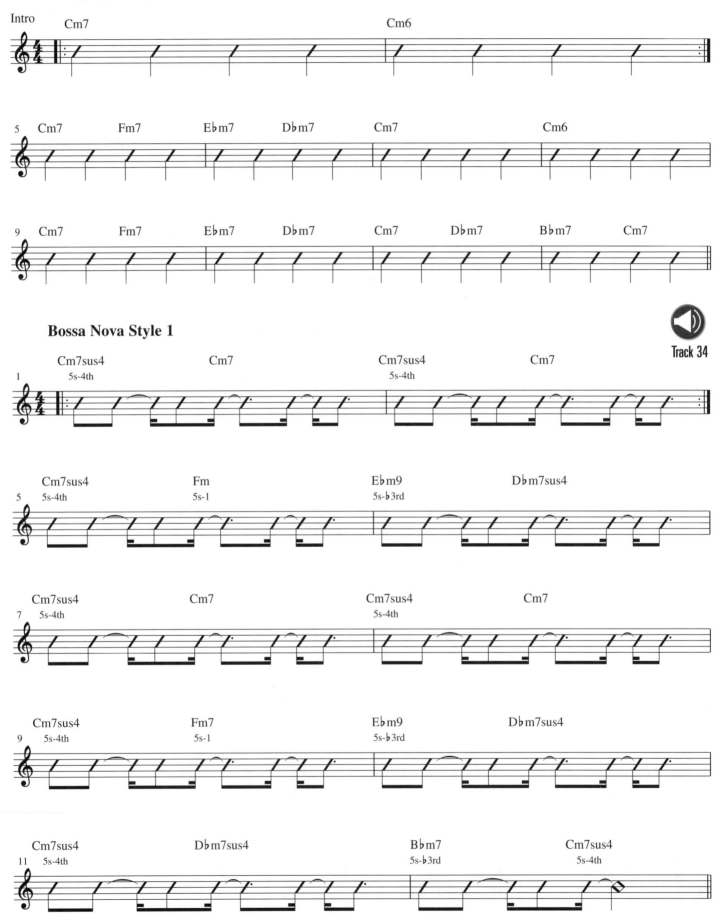

Bossa Nova Style 2–This example is like the previous one except that a bass line has been added. Play the bass line with your thumb and the chords with fingers 1, 2, and 3 of the right hand. Optionally, a flatpick and fingers 2, 3, and 4 can be used.

Track 35

Swing Style 1–"Killer Joe" Rhythm: Charleston-Style Variation

Track 36

Swing Style 2–Four-to-the-Bar Style

In this style we play a chord on each beat of the measure. Also, we want to to play each chord without sounding the note on the B string. This is reminiscent of the Freddie Green style. Mr. Green played with the Count Basie Orchestra and was often called "Mr. Rhythm."

Track 37

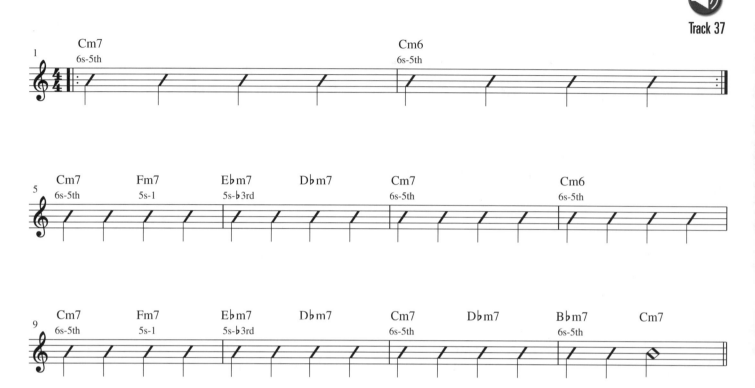

Ballad Style

Play this as smoothly and as pretty as you can!

Track 38

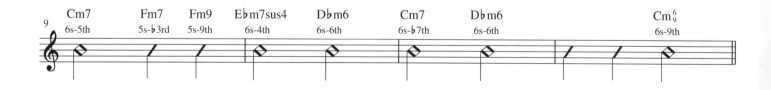

Dominant Chord Formula and Discussion

In order to construct the dominant chords, we have to follow the formulas for each chord. The formulas use the numbered Mixolydian mode and the Lydian ♭7 scales as shown below:

C Mixolydian Mode–Mode 5 of the F Major Scale:

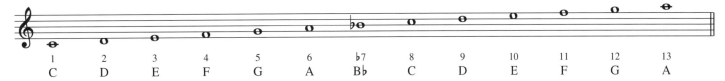

1	2	3	4	5	6	♭7	8	9	10	11	12	13
C	D	E	F	G	A	B♭	C	D	E	F	G	A

C Lydian ♭7 Scale–Mode 4 of the G Melodic Minor Scale:

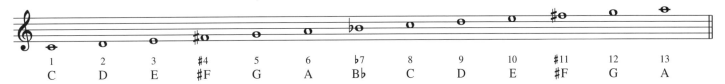

1	2	3	#4	5	6	♭7	8	9	10	#11	12	13
C	D	E	#F	G	A	B♭	C	D	E	#F	G	A

Or, referring to the chord tone chart:

Scale tone	Common name
1	Root or tonic
2	Second
3	Third
4	Fourth
5	Fifth
6	Sixth
♭7	Flatted Seventh
8	Octave
9	Ninth
10	Tenth, octave above Third
11	Eleventh, octave above Fourth
12	Twelfth, octave above Fifth (Not referred to often in jazz)
13	Thirteenth, octave above Sixth

The chord formulas are then constructed basically from "stacking thirds," using every other note of the scale. Study the table below:

Name	Formula	Notes in C	Chord symbol for C
Dominant Seventh	root, 3rd, 5th, ♭7th	C, E, G, B♭	C7
Sus 4	root, 4th, 5th, ♭7th	C, F, G, B♭	C7sus4
Add Sixth	root, 3rd, 5th, 6th, ♭7th	C, E, G, A, B♭	C7(add6)
Ninth	root, 3rd, 5th, ♭7th, 9th	C, E, G, B♭, D	C9
Ninth Sus4	root, 4th, 5th, ♭7th, 9th	C, F, G, B♭, D	C9sus4
Eleventh	root, 3rd, 5th, ♭7th, 9th, 11th	C, E, G, B♭, D, F	C11
Nine Sharp Eleventh	root, 3rd, 5th, ♭7th, 9th, #11th,	C, E, G, B♭, D, F♯	C9#11
Thirteenth	root, 3rd, 5th, ♭7th, 9th, 13th	C, E, G, B♭, D, A	C13
Thirteen Sharp Eleventh	root, 3rd, 5th, ♭7th, 9th, #11th, 13th	C, E, G, B♭, D, F♯, A	C13#11

DOMINANT CHORDS—SEVENTH AND EXTENDED

Track 39

60

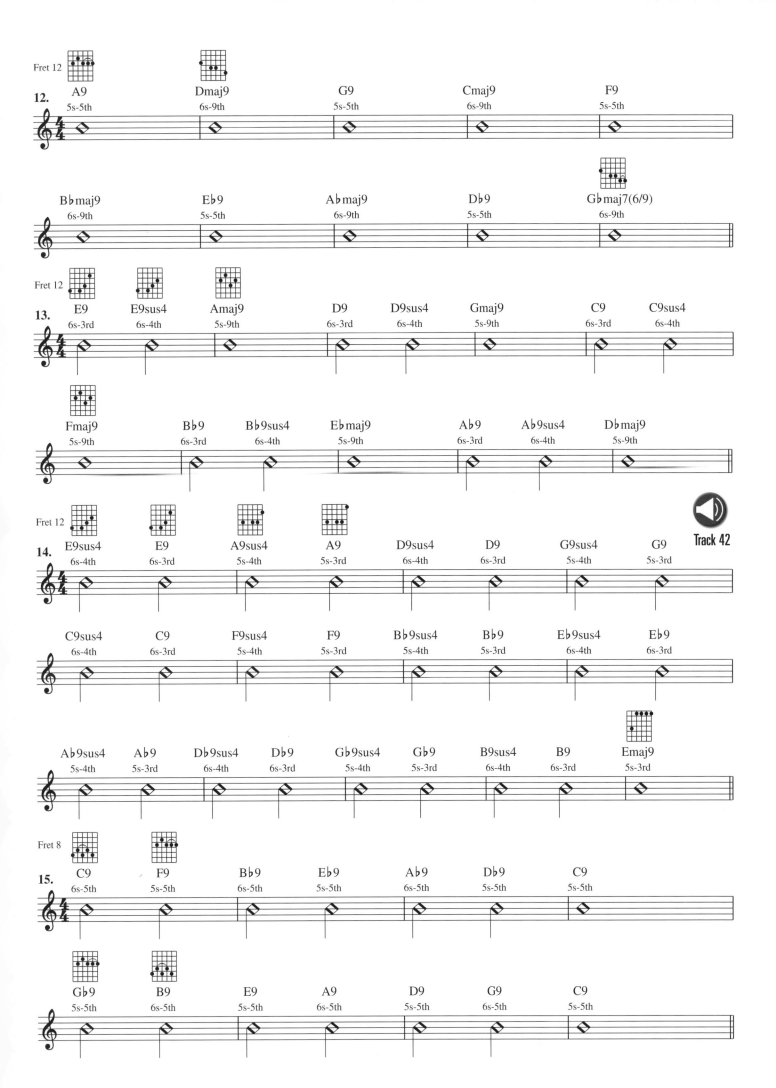

Applications for Dominant

CHORD FAMILY APPROACH

C Mixolydian Scale using Chord Family Approach—Play this a few times, then proceed to the exercises.

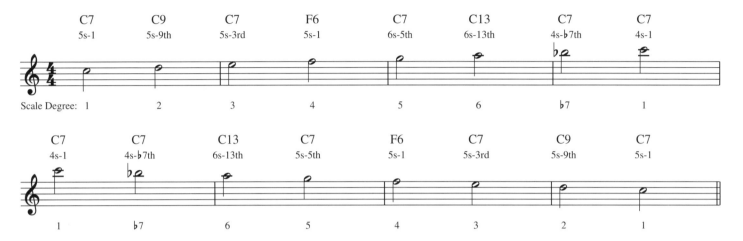

Chord Melody/Chord Solo Exercises for Chord Family Approach—Play the appropriate chord for each note of the melodies below, based on the scale above.

1.

2.

CHORD PAIR APPROACH

In the scale below, a diminished chord is added for color. However, in the exercises, the diminished chord will not be used. (This creates the "Be-Bop" version of the scale.)

C Mixolydian Scale using Chord Pair Approach—Play this a few times, then proceed to the exercises.

Chord Melody/Chord Solo Exercises for Chord Pair Approach—Play the appropriate chord for each note of the melodies below, based on the scale above.

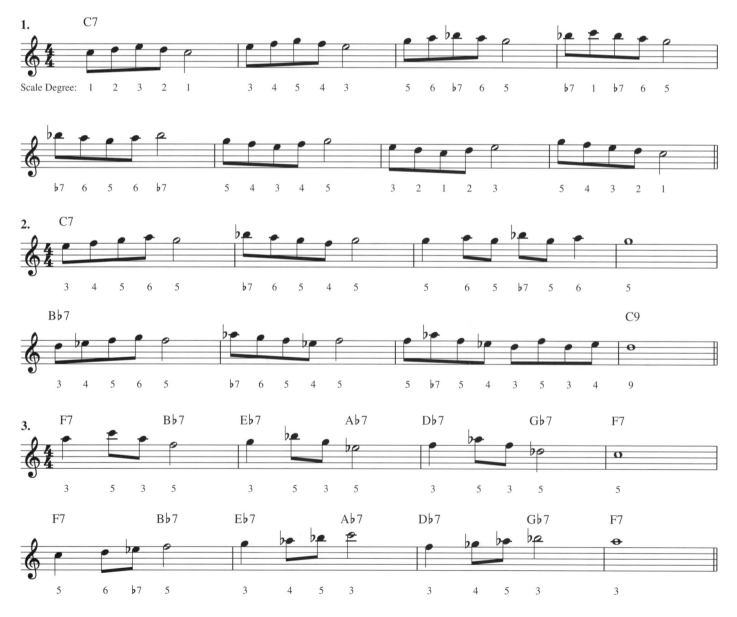

ALTERNATING CHORD/NOTE STYLE

C Mixolydian Mode in Alternating Chord/Note Style—Play this a few times, then proceed to the exercises.

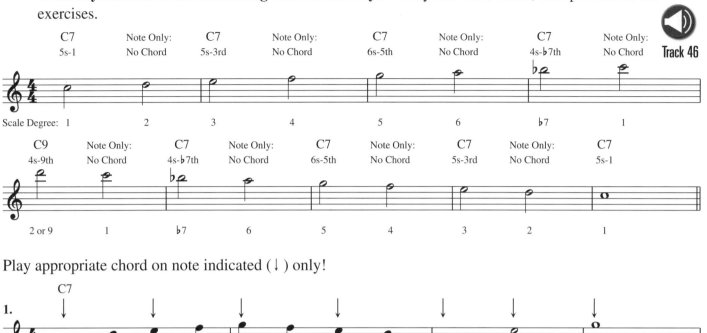

Play appropriate chord on note indicated (↓) only!

COMPING SECTION

Given the example chord progression below, we will apply different styles to it using chords studied thus far. Each comping style is indicated with the corresponding exercise.

Comping Study Progression

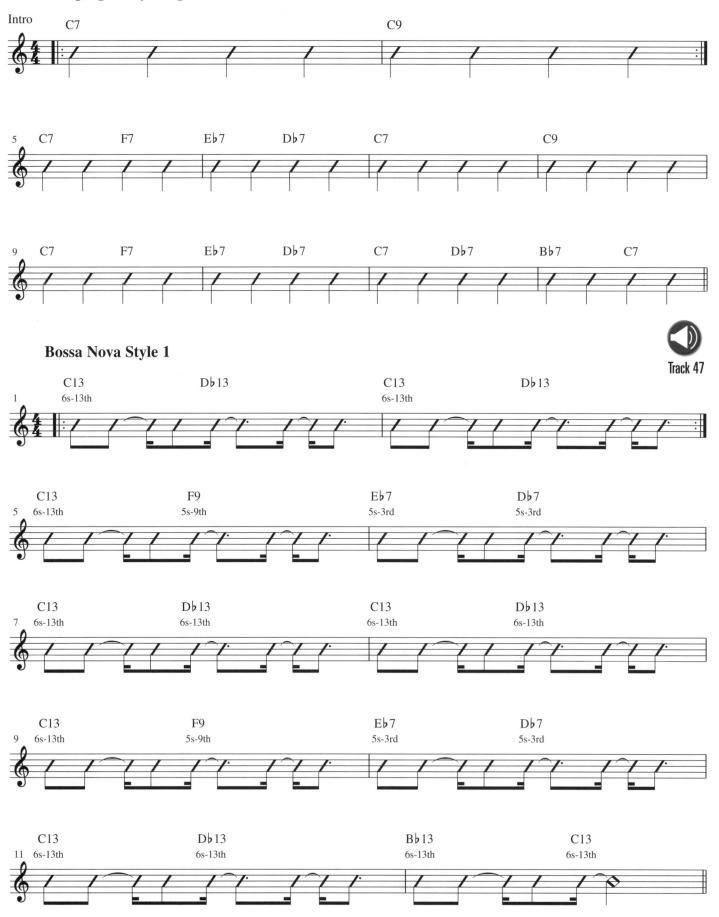

Bossa Nova Style 1

Bossa Nova Style 2–This example is like the previous one except that a bass line has been added. Play the bass line with your thumb and the chords with fingers 1, 2, and 3 of the right hand. Optionally, a flatpick and fingers 2, 3, and 4 can be used.

Swing Style 1–"Killer Joe" Rhythm: Charleston-Style Variation

Track 48

Track 49

Swing Style 2–Four-to-the-Bar Style

In this style we play a chord on each beat of the measure. Also, we want to to play each chord without sounding the note on the B string. This is reminiscent of the Freddie Green style. Mr. Green played with the Count Basie Orchestra and was often called "Mr. Rhythm."

Track 50

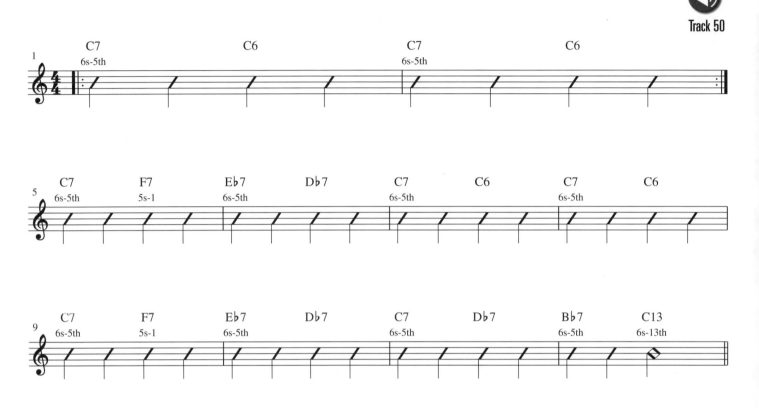

Ballad Style–Play it pretty!

Track 51

Altered Dominant Chord Formula and Discussion

In order to construct altered dominant chords, we have to follow the formulas for each chord. The formulas use altered 5th and 9th tones of the respective scales. The term *altered* means to raise or lower a chord tone by a half step.

C Altered Dominant Scale–Mode 7 of Melodic Minor:

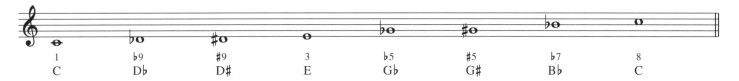

| 1 | ♭9 | #9 | 3 | ♭5 | #5 | ♭7 | 8 |
| C | D♭ | D# | E | G♭ | G# | B♭ | C |

C Auxilliary Diminished Scale–Diminished Half-Whole Scale:

| 1 | ♭9 | #9 | 3 | #4 | 5 | 6 | ♭7 | 8 |
| C | D♭ | D# | E | F# | G | A | B♭ | C |

Or, referring to the chord tone chart:

Chord tone	Common name
1	Root or tonic
♭9	Flatted Ninth
#9	Sharp Nine
3	Third
♭5	Flatted Fifth
#5	Sharp Five
6/13	Sixth or Thirteenth
♭7	Flatted Seventh
8	Octave

The chord formulas are then constructed basically from "stacking thirds," i.e. using every other note of the scale. Study the table below:

Name	Formula	Notes in C	Chord symbol for C
Seventh Flat Fifth	root, 3rd, ♭5th, ♭7th	C, E, G♭, B♭	C7♭5
Seventh Sharp Fifth	root, 3rd, #5th, ♭7th	C, E, G#, B♭	C+7
Seventh Flat Ninth	root, 3rd, 5th, ♭7th, ♭9th	C, E, G, B♭, D♭	C7♭9
Seventh Sharp Ninth	root, 3rd, 5th, ♭7th, #9th	C, E, G, B♭, D#	C7#9
Ninth Flat Fifth	root, 3rd, ♭5th, ♭7th, 9th	C, E, G♭, B♭, D	C9♭5
Ninth Sharp Fifth	root, 3rd, #5th, ♭7th, 9th	C, E, G#, B♭, D	C+9
Seventh Flat Fifth, Flat Ninth	root, 3rd, ♭5th, ♭7th, ♭9th	C, E, G♭, B♭, D♭	C7 ♭9♭5
Seventh Flat Fifth, Sharp Ninth	root, 3rd, ♭5th, ♭7th, #9th	C, E, G♭, B♭, D#	C7 #9♭5
Seventh Sharp Fifth, Flat Ninth	root, 3rd, #5th, ♭7th, ♭9th	C, E, G#, B♭, D♭	C7 ♭9#5
Seventh Sharp Fifth, Sharp Ninth	root, 3rd, #5th, ♭7th, #9th	C, E, G#, B♭, D#	C7 #9#5

AUGMENTED TRIADS—ONE NOTE DOUBLED

Triads, by definition, contain only three different notes. These exercises use four-note voicings in which the fourth note is created by doubling one of the triad notes and either raising or lowering it an octave. The augmented triad is included here because it is most often used as a V+7 chord that resolves to a major or minor I chord.

DOMINANT 7♯5 CHORDS

DOMINANT 7♭5 CHORDS

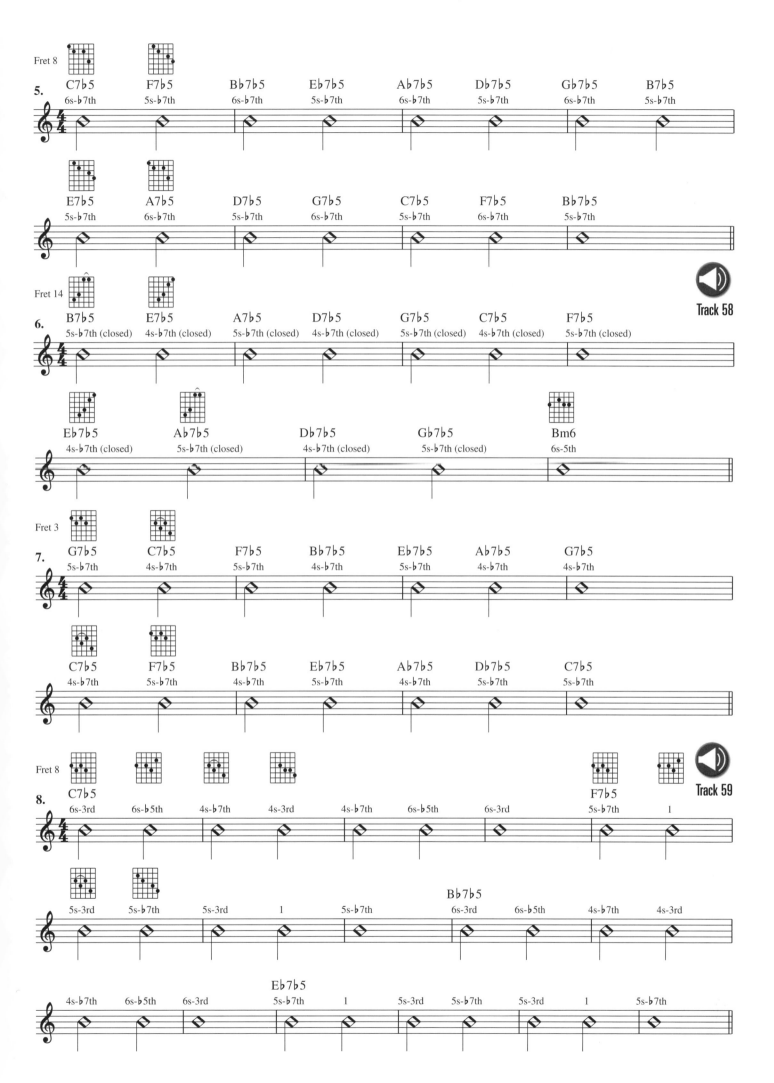

ALTERED DOMINANT CHORDS—SEVENTH AND EXTENDED

79

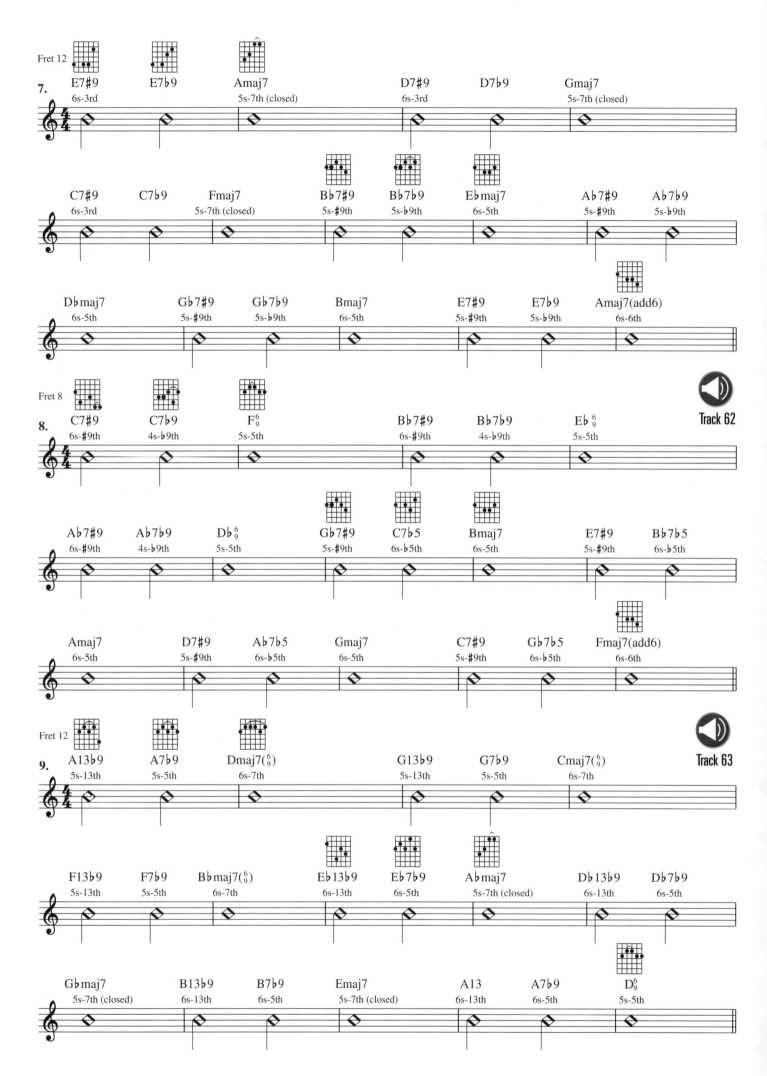

Track 64

81

Applications for Altered Dominant

CHORD FAMILY APPROACH

There are a wide variety of altered dominant chords. To cover them all is beyond the scope of this book. However, the scale below works for altered dominants that contain a raised or a lowered 5th and 9th.

C Altered Dominant Scale using Chord Family Approach—Play this a few times then proceed to the exercises.

Track 65

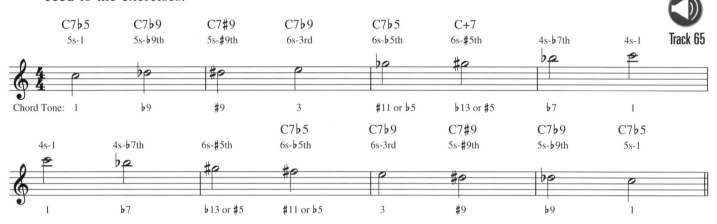

Chord Melody/Chord Solo Exercises for Chord Family Approach—Play the appropriate chord for each note of the melodies below, based on the scale above.

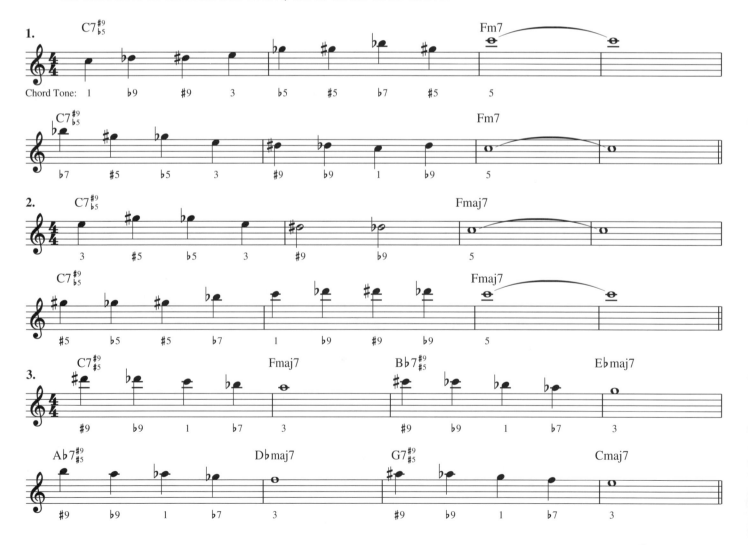

ALTERNATING CHORD/NOTE STYLE

C Altered Dominant Scale in Alternating Chord/Note Style—Play this through, then proceed to the exercises.

Play appropriate chord on note indicated (↓) only!

1.

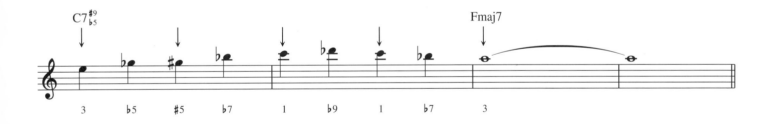

2.

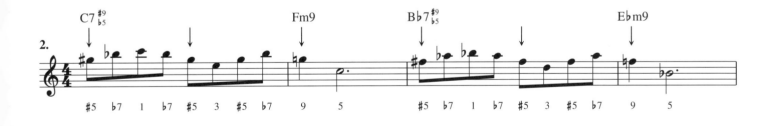

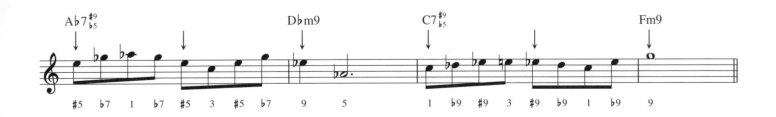

THE WHOLE TONE SCALE

Another scale often used with altered dominants that have either a raised or lowered 5th is the Whole Tone scale. The scale is constructed by using whole steps (i.e., notes 2 frets apart) in succession from a given note until we reach the octave. This is a six note scale. An unaltered second degree (or ninth) means that this scale will only work for chords with an unaltered ninth.

Dominant 7♭5

The symmetrical construction of the scale allows chords derived from the scale to move in a parallel manner. In the example above, we can play the first chord voicing and move it up the neck without changing the chord form or fingering. Notice that when we get to the fourth degree of the scale, we're at C7♭5 again, which is also F♯7♭5. This is also known as a "tritone" relationship because F♯ is a tritone away from C. Also notice that the 3rd and ♭7 of C7 are the ♭7 and 3rd of F♯7.

Augmented Triad

In the next example, we take an augmented triad up the scale. In doing this, we see that the original triad is inverted at every other scale degree. In other words, as we move up the scale, there will be C augmented triads at the 1st, 3rd, and 5th degrees of the scale. Also remember that any note in an augmented triad can be a root!

Dominant 7♯5

Lastly, in the example above, we're taking two chords up the scale. Interestingly enough C7♯5 and D7♯5 can move up the whole tone scale together and spell out the harmony of the scale. Many other combinations of chords are possible! Experiment!

Minor 7♭5 Chord Formula and Discussion

In order to construct minor 7♭5 chords, we have to follow the formulas. The formulas are derived from either the Locrian mode or Mode 6 of the melodic minor scale as shown below:

Locrian Mode–Mode 7 of the Major Scale:

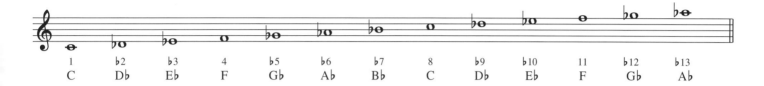

1	♭2	♭3	4	♭5	♭6	♭7	8	♭9	♭10	11	♭12	♭13
C	D♭	E♭	F	G♭	A♭	B♭	C	D♭	E♭	F	G♭	A♭

Locrian #2 Mode–Mode 6 of the Melodic Minor Scale:

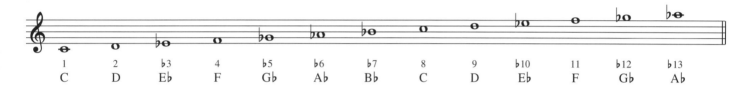

1	2	♭3	4	♭5	♭6	♭7	8	9	♭10	11	♭12	♭13
C	D	E♭	F	G♭	A♭	B♭	C	D	E♭	F	G♭	A♭

Or, referring to the chord tone chart:

Chord tone	Common name
1	Root or tonic
♭3	Flatted Third or Minor Third
♭5	Flatted Fifth
♭7	Flatted Seventh
9	Ninth
11	Eleventh, octave above Fourth

The chord formulas are then constructed basically from "stacking thirds," i.e. using every other note of the scale. Study the table below:

Name	Formula	Notes in C	Chord symbol for C
Minor Seventh Flat Five	root, ♭3rd, ♭5th, ♭7th	C, E♭, G♭, B♭	Cm7♭5
Minor Ninth Flat Five	root, ♭3rd, ♭5th, ♭7th, 9th	C, E♭, G♭, B♭, D	Cm9♭5
Minor Eleventh Flat Five	root, ♭3rd, ♭5th, ♭7th, 9th, 11th	C, E♭, G♭, B♭, D, F	Cm11♭5

You'll notice that the scale used in the upcoming Alternating Chord/Note Style section is different from the Locrian scale shown above. Without going into a lengthy explanation of modes and scales, it's helpful to point out that the two most popular scale choices for a minor 7♭5 chord are:

1. Locrian Mode—mode 7 of the major scale
2. Locrian #2 Mode—mode 6 of the melodic minor scale

MINOR 7♭5 CHORDS—SEVENTH AND EXTENDED

Applications for Minor 7♭5

CHORD FAMILY APPROACH

In the scale below, a diminished chord is added for color. However, in the exercises, the diminished chord will not be used.

C Minor 7♭5 Scale using Chord Family Approach

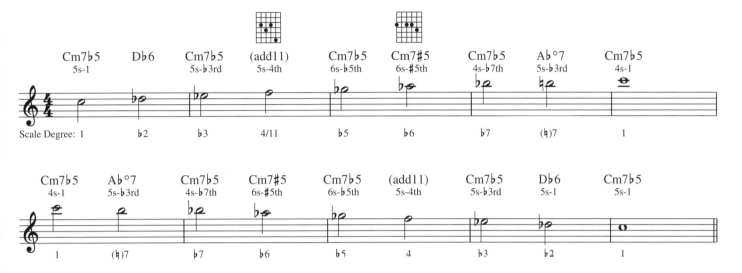

Chord Melody/Chord Solo Exercises for Chord Family Approach—Play the appropriate chord for each note of the melodies below, based on the scale above.

1.

2.

CHORD PAIR APPROACH

C Minor 7♭5 Scale or C Locrian using Chord Pair Approach

In the scale below, a diminished chord is added for color. However, in the exercises, the diminished chord will not be used.

Play the scale below a few times before proceeding to the exercises.

Chord Melody/Chord Solo Exercises for Chord Pair Approach—Play the appropriate chord for each note of the melodies below, based on the scale above.

ALTERNATING CHORD/NOTE STYLE

C Minor 7♭5 Scale in Alternating Chord/Note Style

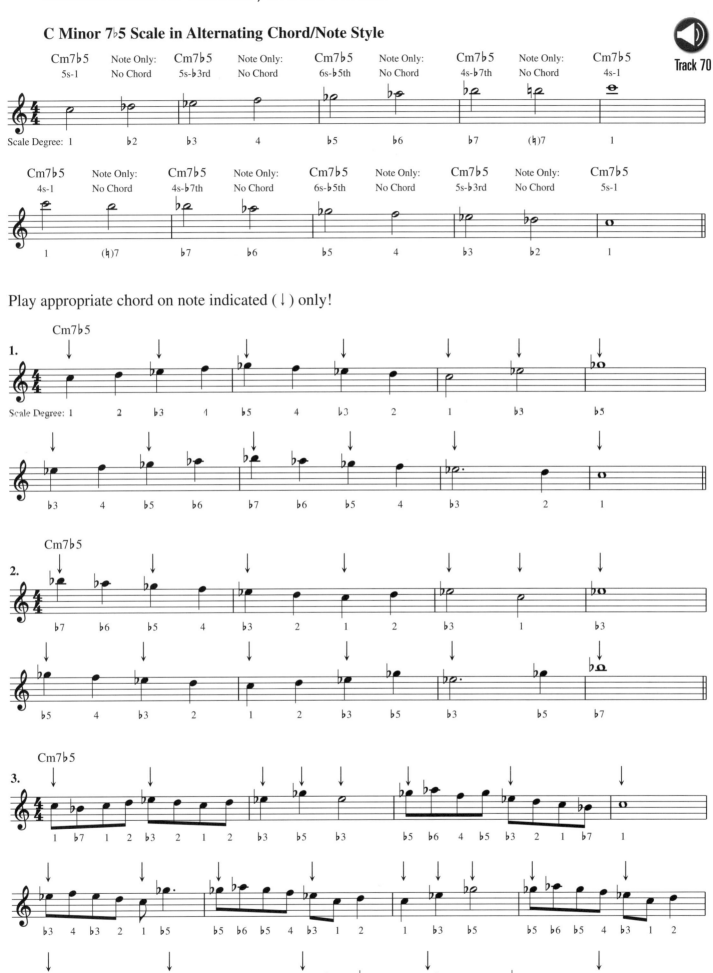

Play appropriate chord on note indicated (↓) only!

Diminished Chord Formula and Discussion

In order to construct diminished chords, we have to follow the formulas. The formulas use the diminished scale as seen below:

C Diminished Scale:

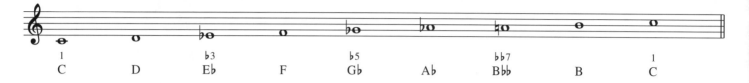

1		♭3		♭5		♭♭7		1
C	D	E♭	F	G♭	A♭	B♭♭	B	C

Or, referring to the chord tone chart:

Chord tone	Common name
1	Root or tonic
♭3	Flatted Third
♭5	Flatted Fifth
♭♭7	Double Flatted Seventh—Same Note as Sixth

The chord formulas are then constructed basically from "stacking thirds," i.e. using every other note of the scale. Study the table below:

Name	Formula	Notes in C	Chord symbol for C
Diminished Triad	root, ♭3rd, ♭5th	C, E♭, G♭	C°
Diminished Seventh	root, ♭3rd, ♭5th, ♭♭7th	C, E♭, G♭, B♭♭	C°7

Additionally, diminished chords can be extended by adding a note one whole step above any chord tone; e.g., add the scale tone between two consecutive chord tones.

DIMINISHED CHORDS—SEVENTH

95

Applications for Diminished

CHORD FAMILY APPROACH

C Diminished Scale using Chord Family Approach

Every note in a diminished 7th chord can be a root. Diminished chords are inverted by moving the voicing up or down a minor 3rd (3 frets). So, in the scale below, which is a harmonized diminished scale, every other chord has the same notes. So, C°7 has the same notes as E♭°7, F♯°7, and A°7.

Also, diminished chords can be extended in either of 2 ways:
1. Adding a note that is one whole step above any chord tone
2. Adding a note that is one half step below any chord tone

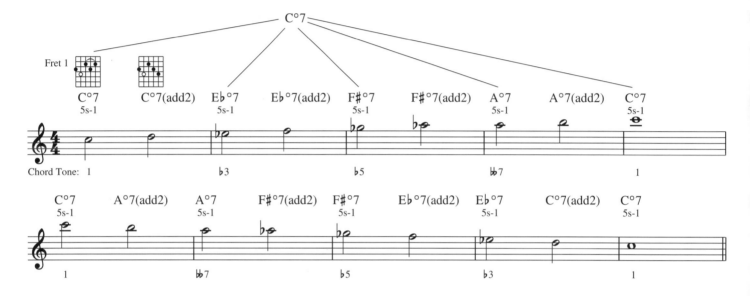

Chord Melody/Chord Solo Exercises for Chord Family Approach—Play the appropriate chord for each note of the melodies below, based on the scale above.

96

CHORD PAIR APPROACH

C Diminished Scale using Chord Pair Approach

We can harmonize a diminished scale by pairing a given diminished chord with another diminished chord either a whole step above, or a half step below the first diminished chord. For example, a C diminished scale can be harmonized by using C°7 and D°7, or C°7 and B°7. Remember that every note in a diminished 7th chord can be a root. Also, remember that diminished chords can be inverted by moving a given voicing up or down in minor 3rd intervals (3 frets).

So, C°7 has the same notes as E♭°7, G♭°7, and A°7. Likewise, D°7 has the same notes as F°7, A♭°7, and B°7.

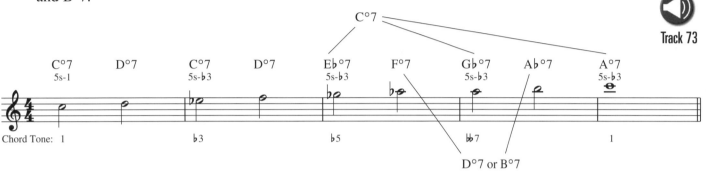

Chord Melody/Chord Solo Exercises for Chord Pair Approach—Play the appropriate chord for each note of the melodies below, based on the scale above.

ALTERNATING CHORD/NOTE STYLE

C Diminished Scale in Alternating Chord/Note Style—Note: these chords are all inversions of C°7.

Track 74

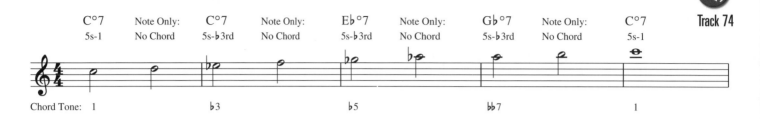

Play appropriate chord on note indicated (↓) only!

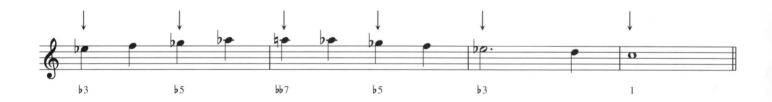

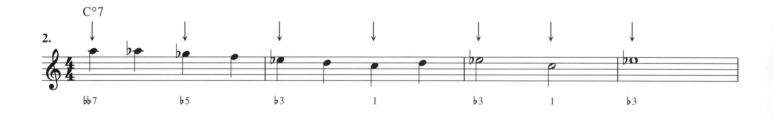

DIMINISHED SCALE & DOMINANT 7♭9 CHORDS

The diminished chord and scale can both be used with dominant 7♭9 chords. Let's look at a C diminished scale as shown below with chord tones indicated.

Scale Degree: Root   ♭3   #4/♭5   6/♭♭7   Root

Now, take a look at the notes in a B7♭9 chord (shown below).

Chord Tone: Root   3rd   5th   ♭7   ♭9

Notice that the B7♭9 chord tones are all contained in the C diminished scale. Finally, if we take the C diminished scale and start on the note B, it then follows that this scale fits a B7♭9 chord.

Scale Degree: Root   ♭9   #9   3rd   #4   5th   6th   7th   Root   ♭9

This means that we can use our harmonized C diminished scale over a B7♭9 chord. As a matter of fact, this scale works for B7♭9, D7♭9, F7♭9, and A♭7♭9. In the example below, we have a B7♭9 in the first bar resolving to an E$^6_9$ chord in the second bar. Using diminished chords moving up the C diminished scale, a pretty melodic passage is created. This example is reminiscent of Wes Montgomery's style.

PART III
Chord Progression Studies

Many chord progressions are based on chords from the harmonized major scale. For example, building chords from the C major scale means stacking scale tones on top of each note in the scale until we get chords—i.e., triads, seventh chords, or ninth chords. We stack the notes in 3rds. To put it another way, for a given note in the scale, we add notes that are two letter names away from the preceding note. See below:

Stacking 3rds on the C Major Scale:

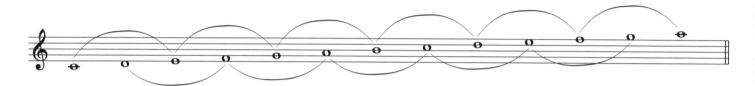

After stacking 3rds on each scale degree, we end up with seven chords as shown below. Keep in mind that we're using the C major scale as an example. The same approach will work for all keys. A definite pattern can be seen. Namely, there are:

    a) 2 Major 7th Chords–Cmaj7, Fmaj7

    b) 3 Minor 7th Chords–Dm7, Em7, Am7

    c) 1 Dominant 7th Chord–G7

    d) 1 Minor 7♭5 Chord–Bm7♭5

Harmonized C Major:

Imaj7	IIm7	IIIm7	IVmaj7	V7	VIm7	VIIm7♭5
Cmaj7	Dm7	Em7	Fmaj7	G7	Am7	Bm7♭5

HARMONIZED SCALES

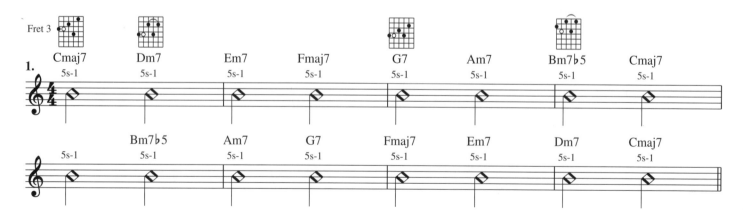

100

Two–Five–One: Formula and Discussion

It is common to refer to the chords in the harmonized scale by number. The exercises in this section will utilize the 2nd, 5th, and 1st degrees of the major scale—a.k.a. "two, five, one." In the key of C, this is Dm7, G7, and Cmaj7, respectively. The "two–five–one" is one of the most used chord structures in jazz, and as such, you will need to get as comfortable with it as possible.

TWO–FIVES

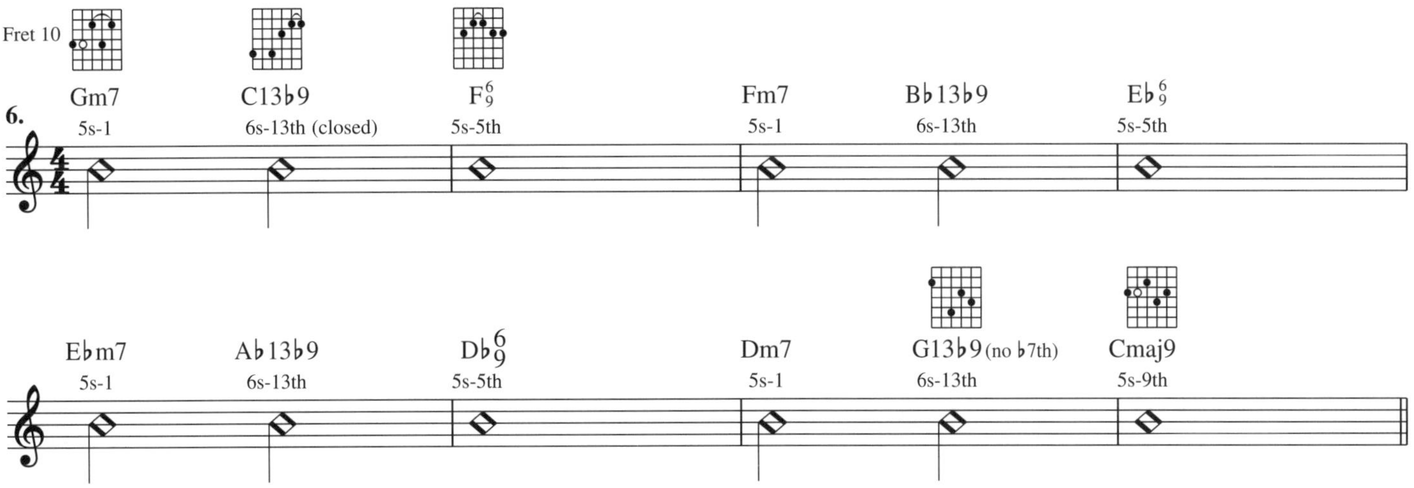
Fret 10
6.
Gm7 5s-1
C13♭9 6s-13th (closed)
F6/9 5s-5th
Fm7 5s-1
B♭13♭9 6s-13th
E♭6/9 5s-5th
E♭m7 5s-1
A♭13♭9 6s-13th
D♭6/9 5s-5th
Dm7 5s-1
G13♭9 (no ♭7th) 6s-13th
Cmaj9 5s-9th

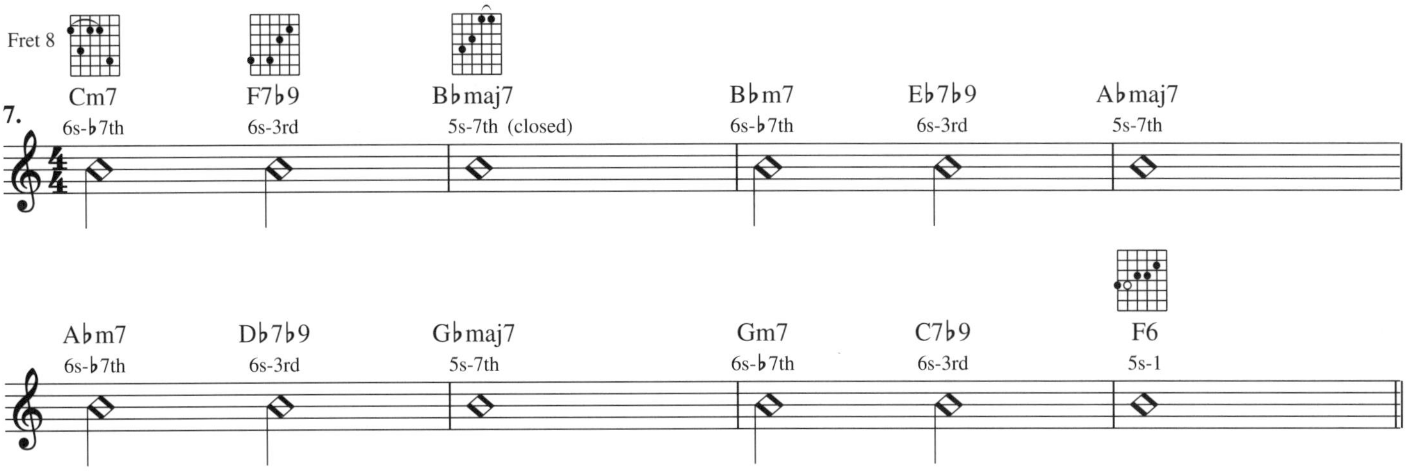
Fret 8
7.
Cm7 6s-♭7th
F7♭9 6s-3rd
B♭maj7 5s-7th (closed)
B♭m7 6s-♭7th
E♭7♭9 6s-3rd
A♭maj7 5s-7th
A♭m7 6s-♭7th
D♭7♭9 6s-3rd
G♭maj7 5s-7th
Gm7 6s-♭7th
C7♭9 6s-3rd
F6 5s-1

Track 82

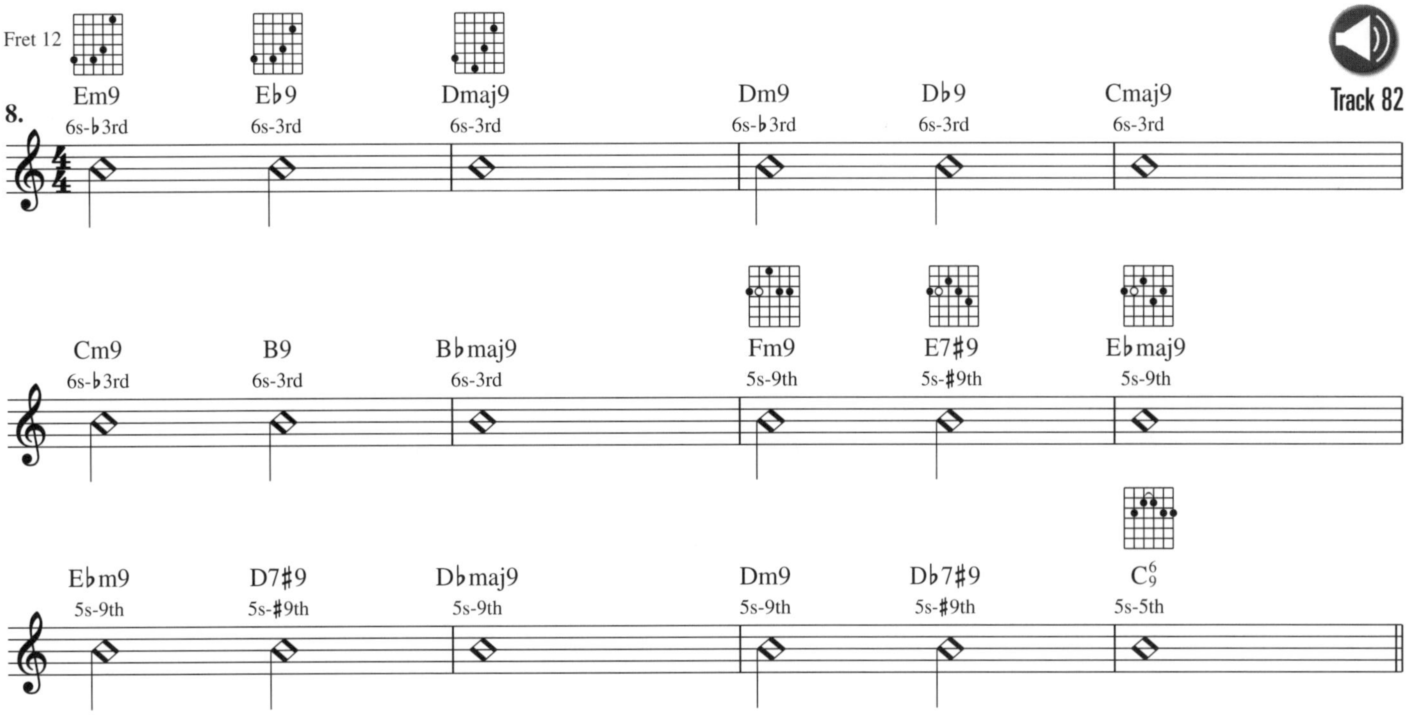
Fret 12
8.
Em9 6s-♭3rd
E♭9 6s-3rd
Dmaj9 6s-3rd
Dm9 6s-♭3rd
D♭9 6s-3rd
Cmaj9 6s-3rd
Cm9 6s-♭3rd
B9 6s-3rd
B♭maj9 6s-3rd
Fm9 5s-9th
E7♯9 5s-♯9th
E♭maj9 5s-9th
E♭m9 5s-9th
D7♯9 5s-♯9th
D♭maj9 5s-9th
Dm9 5s-9th
D♭7♯9 5s-♯9th
C6/9 5s-5th

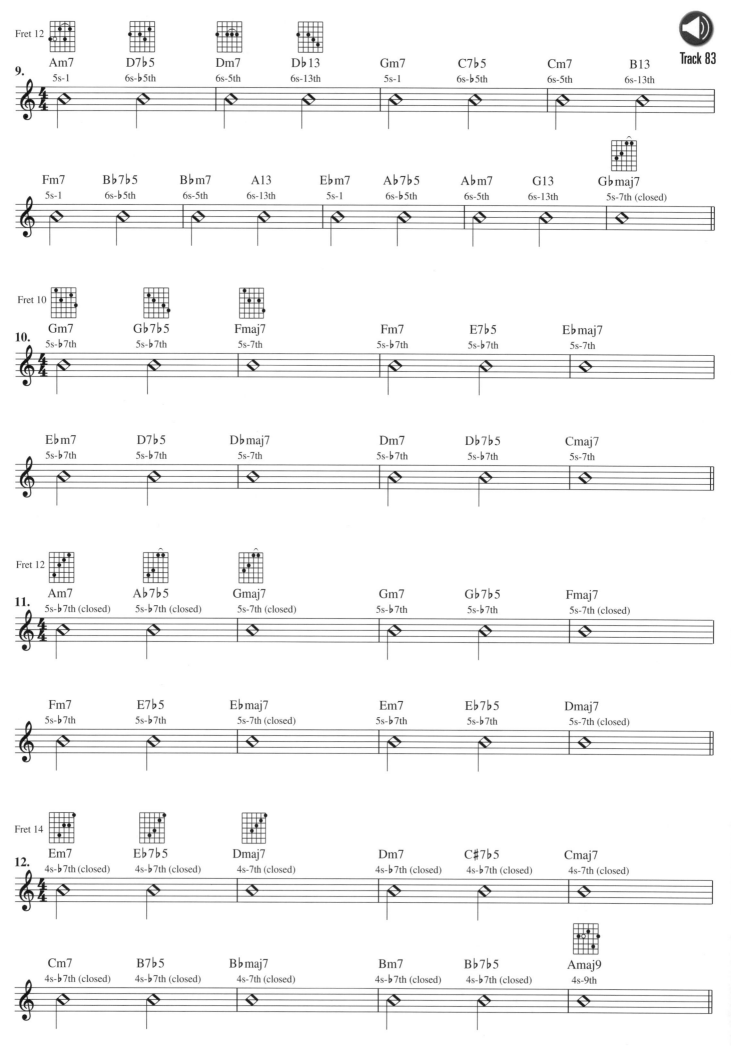

Minor Two–Five–One: Formula and Discussion

Like its major counterparts, the minor two–five and two–five–one are also popular in jazz. Below, you will see the three most popular minor scales used in jazz: the pure or natural minor, the melodic minor, and the harmonic minor. The chords derived from each scale are also shown. This was done from "stacking thirds" in each scale. Remember this from the earlier discussion on II–V7–I in major? Jazz composers past and present have freely and creatively used the chords derived from these scales. By drawing on so many chords and harmonies, a wide variety of minor textures have been explored. However, the most common form of the minor II–V7–I is: IIm7♭5–V7♭9–Im7, Im6, or Im(maj7). Comparing the harmonized scales below, you can see that the harmonic minor scale contains a IIm7♭5, a V7♭9, and a Im(maj7). However, many jazz composers mix chords from either or all of these and other scales.

C Natural Minor Scale:

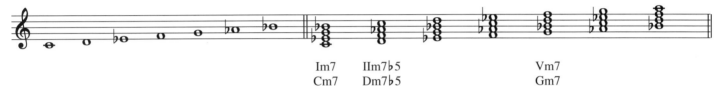

Im7	IIm7♭5		Vm7
Cm7	Dm7♭5		Gm7

C Melodic Minor Scale:

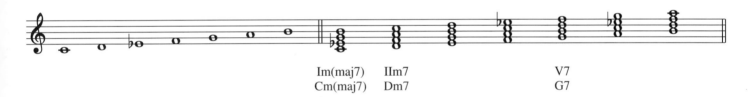

Im(maj7)	IIm7		V7
Cm(maj7)	Dm7		G7

C Harmonic Minor Scale:

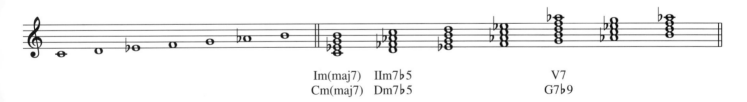

Im(maj7)	IIm7♭5		V7
Cm(maj7)	Dm7♭5		G7♭9

On the V7 chord, we extended it by stacking another 3rd to get the ♭9. The harmonic minor scale is the only one of the three popular minor scales that contains a ♭9th in the V7 chord.

MINOR TWO–FIVES

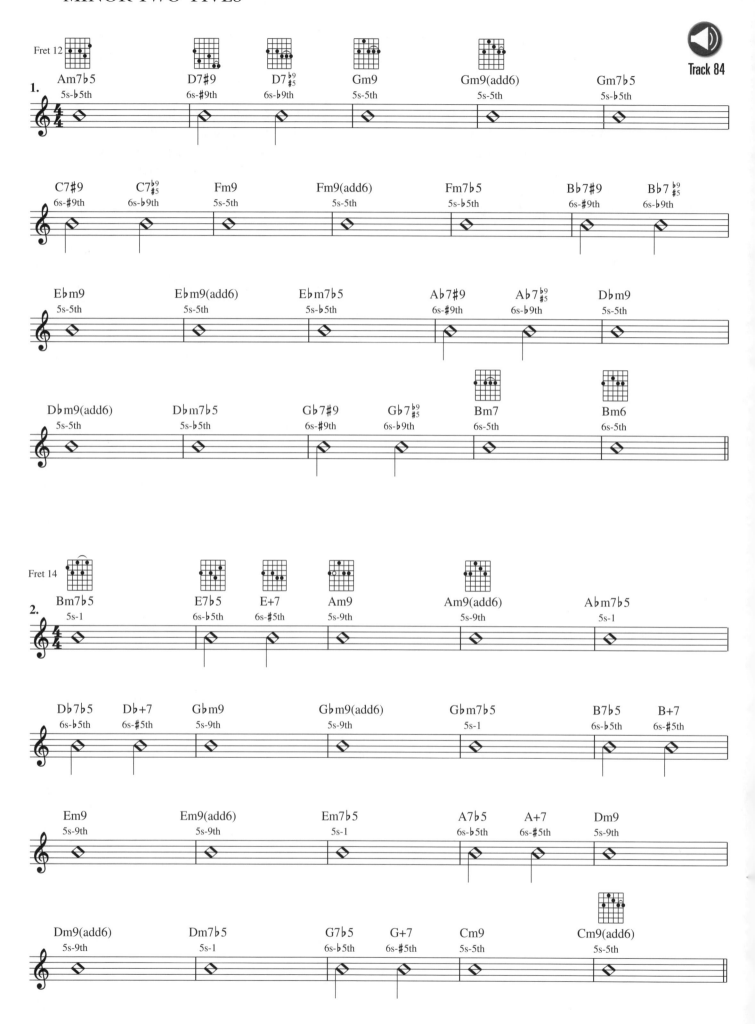

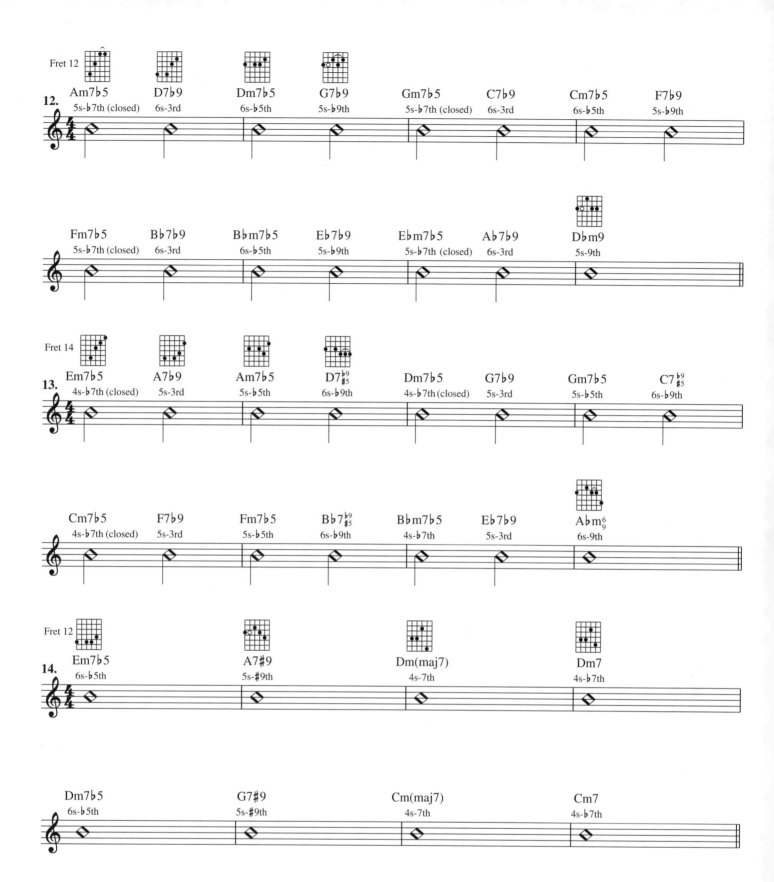

One–Six–Two–Five: Formula and Discussion

Another popular chord progression is the I–VIm7–IIm7–V7 or "one–six–two–five." Again, looking at the harmonized C major scale (see below), this progression in the key of C becomes: Cmaj7–Am7–Dm7–G7.

Hamonized C Major Scale:

Imaj7	IIm7	IIIm7	IVmaj7	V7	VIm7	VIIm7♭5
Cmaj7	Dm7	Em7	Fmaj7	G7	Am7	Bm7♭5

MINOR ONE–SIX–TWO–FIVES

Again, looking at the three popular minor scales, (see below) there are a number of possibilities for a I–VI–II–V in minor. However, the most popular version draws from both the melodic and harmonic minor.

C Natural Minor Scale:

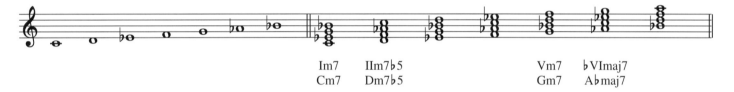

Im7	IIm7♭5			Vm7	♭VImaj7
Cm7	Dm7♭5			Gm7	A♭maj7

C Melodic Minor Scale:

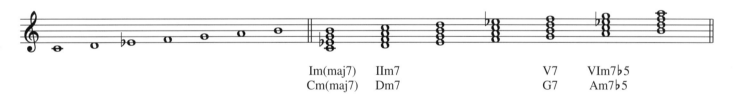

Im(maj7)	IIm7			V7	VIm7♭5
Cm(maj7)	Dm7			G7	Am7♭5

C Harmonic Minor Scale:

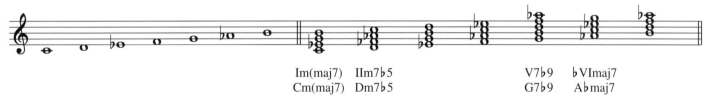

Im(maj7)	IIm7♭5			V7♭9	♭VImaj7
Cm(maj7)	Dm7♭5			G7♭9	A♭maj7

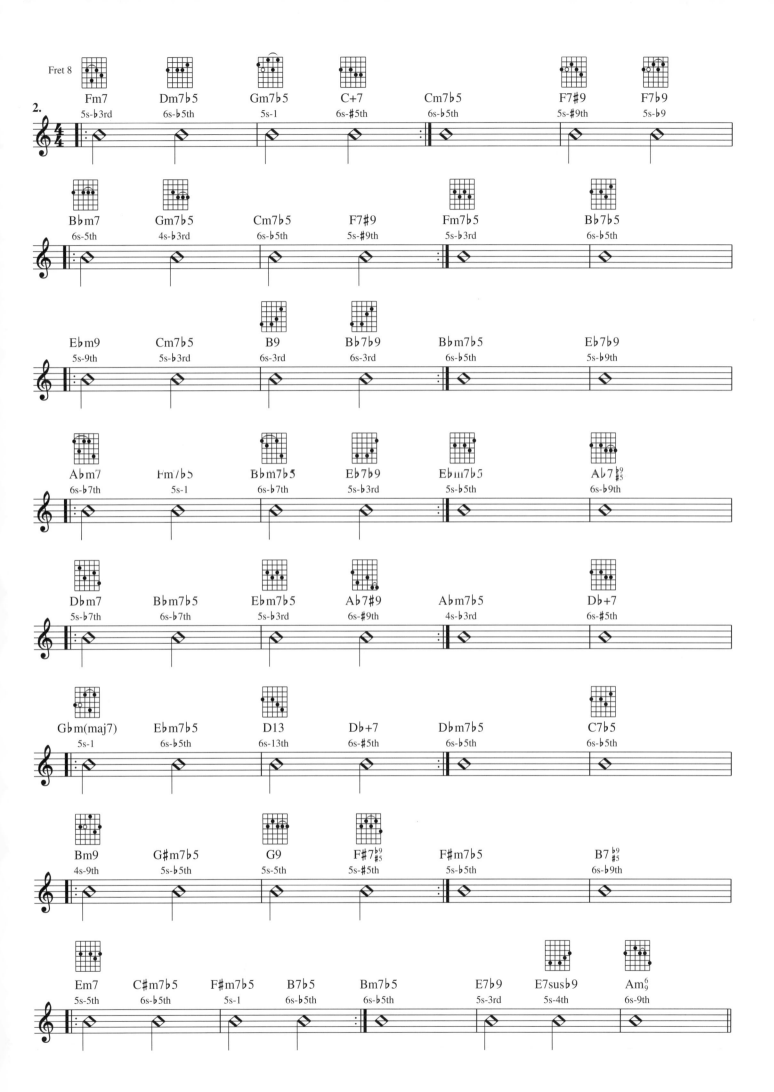

115

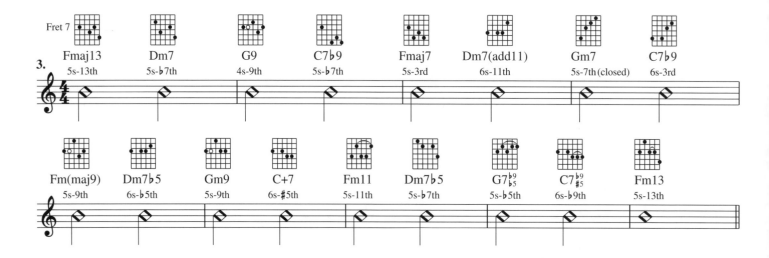

PROGRESSIONS WITH DIMINISHED CHORDS

Diminished chords are most often used as connections or transitions between chords to create interest. See the example below.

The progression above becomes more interesting with the addition of diminished chords in the first two measures.

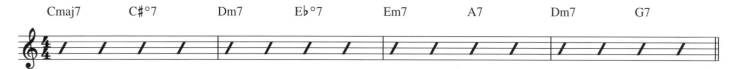

Now try these exercises on progressions with diminished chords.

Track 89

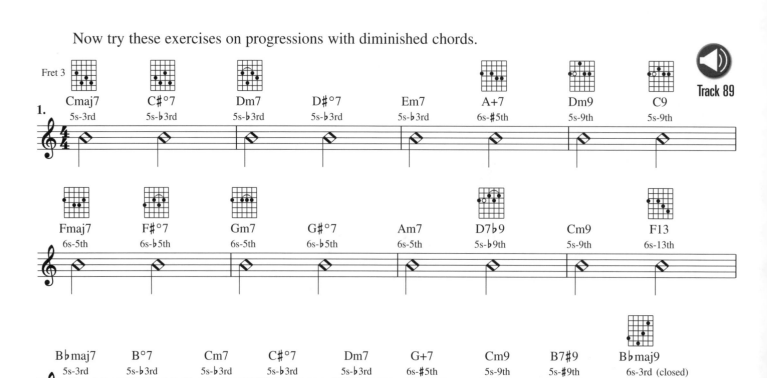

116

PART IV
Puttin' It All Together

Now it's time to go through some song examples and put some of what we've learned to use. Hopefully, by looking at chord charts from actual songs, you will gain insight into how to use what has been learned thus far.

Of course we're looking at the three basic applications for chords:

Comping

In this section we have three example tunes to play. The styles are:

1. Modal Swing–This tune is based on Miles Davis' "So What." The entire tune is just two chords. Therefore it is a challenge to comp effectively without being boring or monotonous.
2. Bossa Nova–This tune is based on the jazz standard "Watch What Happens" by Michele LeGrand. Here we apply the bossa nova styles 1 and 2 from the exercises.
3. Medium Tempo Swing–This is a standard 12-bar blues progression. There are four choruses, and different approaches are taken in each chorus.

Chord Melody

In this section, we look at three actual songs. These songs are in the public domain—free to use because the copyright has expired. The three tunes here demonstrate some of the potential for reharmonization from using voicings in this book. These arrangements rely mostly on the "Chord Family Approach," but, use of the "Chord Pair Approach" can be seen as well.

Chord Soloing

Finally, we look at three chord solos. These three tunes are based on the jazz standards "Misty," "My Foolish Heart," and "Autumn Leaves." The first 2 tunes have solos using the "Chord Pair Approach" from the exercises. The last tune features the "Alternating Chord/Note Style" from the exercises. Hopefully, after learning these solos, you'll go back and improvise your own solos using all the principles that have been studied up to now.

Comping Section

The chord progression below is based on Miles Davis' "So What." Notice that this 32-bar tune has only two chords. This tune is *modal*, which means that the harmony is based on a mode—in this case, the Dorian mode. Take a good look at the basic chord progression and the chord voicings below before proceeding.

MODAL COMP

Basic Chord Progression:

Chord Voicings for This Exercise–Note: Root string is indicated below each diagram and highest chord tone is above each diagram.

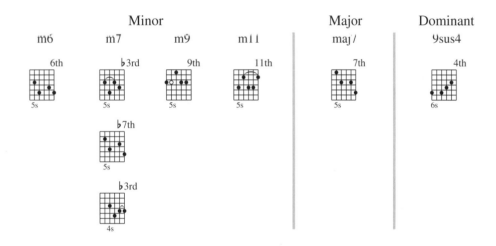

The Form: AABA

Many jazz compositions have been written in a 32-bar format. This means that the entire song is just 32 bars long (also known as a chorus), which then repeats any number of times before the song ends. These 32 bars are further subdivided into groups of eight-bar sections. The first eight bars (a.k.a: section A) normally repeat and then are followed by another eight bars called the bridge. The last eight bars return to the A section again. This form is often called the AABA form and is very common in jazz. In this example, I have designated the sections as follows: A1, A2, B, A3. A good musician is always keenly aware of the form of the tune he or she is playing.

Modal Comp—Study

LOOK TO SEE

This is based on "Watch What Happens" by Michelle Legrand. We're going to apply bossa nova styles 1 and 2 from the exercises. Study the basic progression and the chords that follow before proceeding to the comp exercise.

Basic Chord Progression:

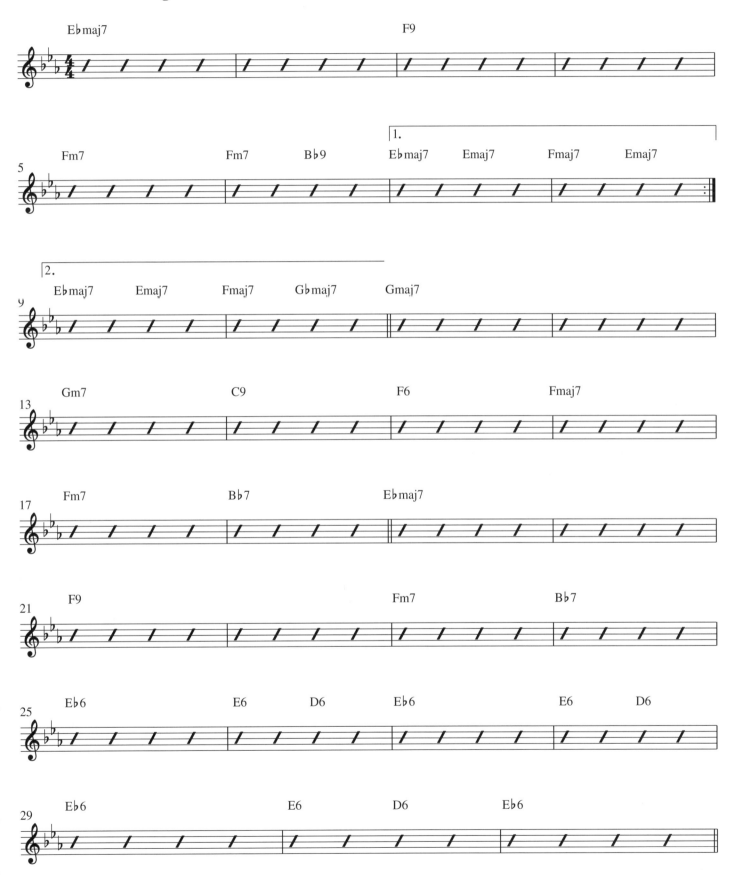

Chord Voicings for This Exercise–Note: Root string is indicated below each diagram and highest chord tone is above each diagram.

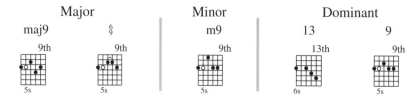

Rhythm Styles for This Exercise

Bossa Nova Style 1

Bossa Nova Style 2–This example is like the previous one except that a bass line has been added. Play the bass line with your thumb and the chords with the fingers 1, 2, and 3 of the right hand. Optionally, a flatpick and fingers 2, 3, and 4 can be used.

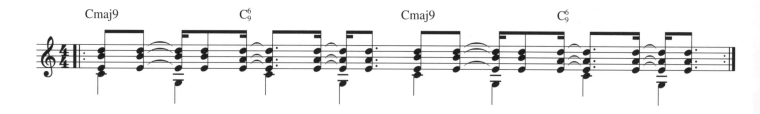

"Look to See"–Comping Study

DA' BLUES

Basic Chord Progression:

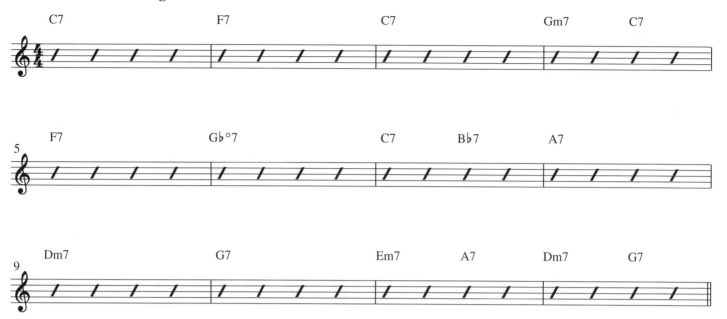

Chord Voicings for This Exercise–Note: Root string is indicated below each diagram and highest chord tone is above each diagram.

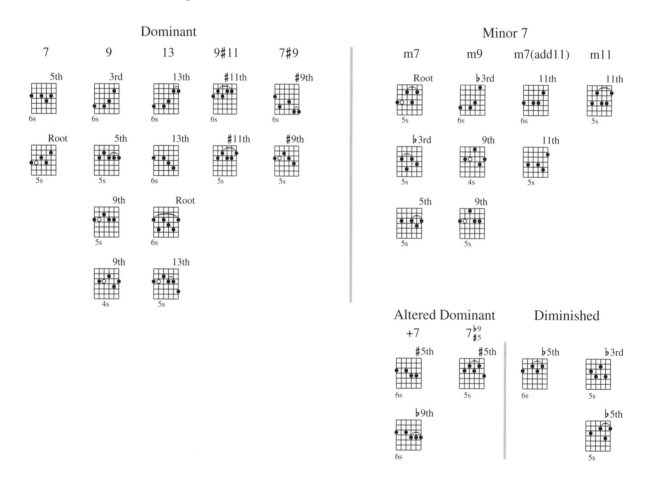

"Da' Blues"–Comping Study

This first chorus is played using Swing Style 2, a.k.a. Freddy Green style. (Refer to Part II.)

Track 92

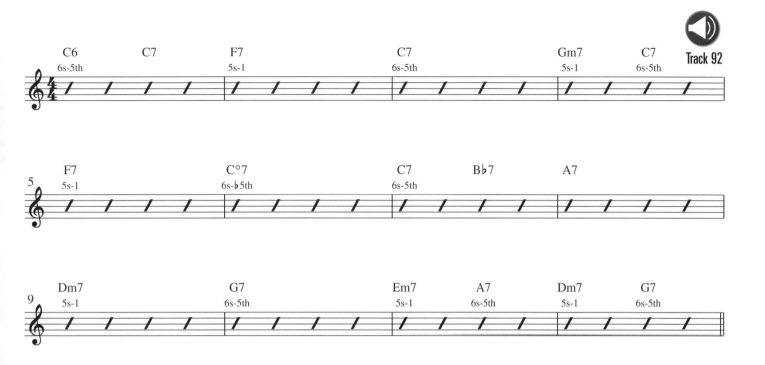

This is Swing Style 2 from the exercises.

Chorus 3 uses rhythms almost like a big band horn section.

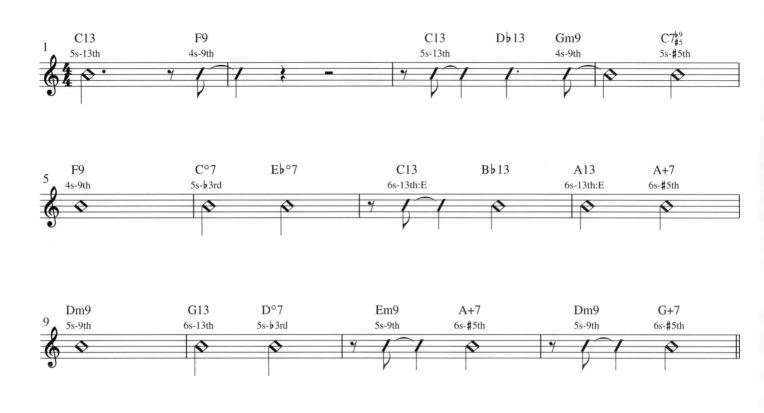

Chorus 4 uses all sustained chords, which can push a soloist if used sparingly.

Chord Melody Section

Now it's time to play some chord melody arrangements. But before we proceed, let's take another look at what chord melody playing is and how it is done. The basic idea is to take a song, i.e., a melody with chord changes, and play the melody with chords. In the earlier sections of this book, we took two approaches to chord melody:

1. Chord Family Approach–which simply means to put a chord from the given chord family on every melody note.

2. Chord Pair Approach–this approach also puts a chord on every note but alternates between two or more chords from different families as you move through a given scale.

3. Alternating Chord/Note Style–In this style, chords and single notes alternate to give an effect similar to the way a jazz piano player uses his or her left hand to comp while the right hand plays the melody.

Also, there is the possibility of reharmonizing the original chord progression to the melody. This means to either create a new progression or to modify the original in a way that adds color and interest without altering the original melody. Reharmonization of chord progressions is a lengthy subject well beyond the scope of this book. In short, I recommend that you listen to as many recordings as possible. Try to figure out the chord progressions to your favorite arrangements. Use what you learn in your own arrangements. If you're in school, take an arranging class or two!

Of course we need some basic guidelines for creating chord melody arrangements:

1. Learn the melody to the point that you can sing or hum it.

2. Learn the chords to the song well enough that you can comp through it without looking at the music.

3. For the arrangement, it may be necessary to take the melody up an octave so that we can have the fullest sounding chords at our disposal. Sometimes changing keys accomplishes the same thing.

4. Identify each note of the melody as it relates to its corresponding chord, i.e. root, 3rd, 5th, etc.

5. Most often, the melody is the top note of each chord, but there are exceptions.

Looking at the example below:

From the first note C, we can see that our options for having a full chord underneath are limited. In fact, if we kept the melody written this low, a chord melody arrangement just wouldn't make any sense.

But, if we take the melody up an octave, we can find some good chords to use. In fact, after studying the chord progression and identifying the relationships of the melody notes to the chords, we can even apply a minor II–V7 substitution.

With all this in mind, we can move on to the exercises...

ROCK-A-BYE BABY

Given the 16-bar lead sheet to "Rock-A-Bye Baby" (below), let's transform it into a nice sounding chord melody arrangement.

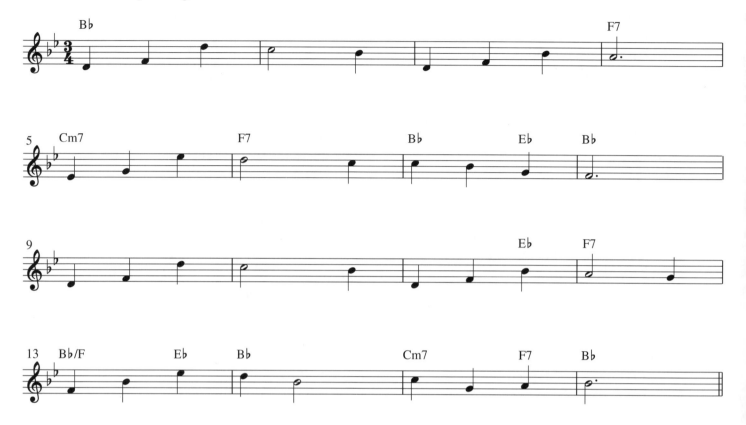

Chord Voicings for This Exercise–Note: Root string is indicated below each diagram and highest chord tone is above each diagram.

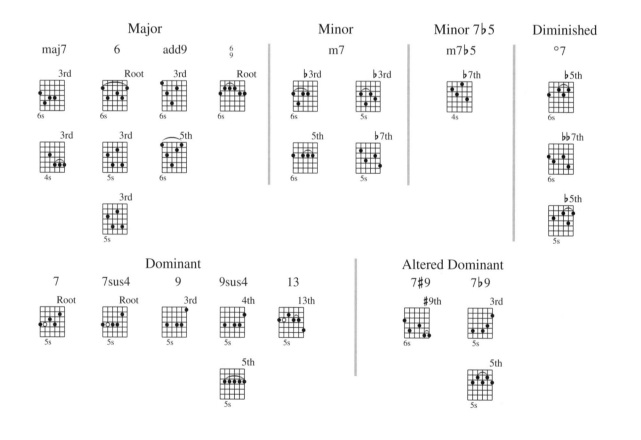

"Rock-A-Bye Baby"–Chord Melody Arrangement

In this arrangement, we're playing the melody an octave higher than written.

Track 93

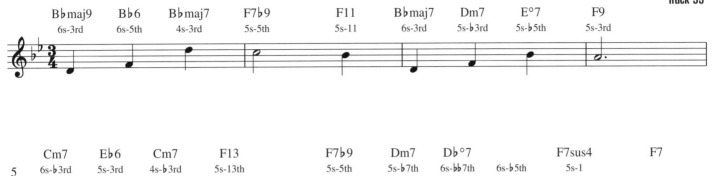

AULD LANG SYNE

Given eight bars from the lead sheet to "Auld Lang Syne" (below), let's transform it into a chord melody arrangement.

Chord Voicings for This Exercise–Note: Root string is indicated below each diagram and highest chord tone is above each diagram.

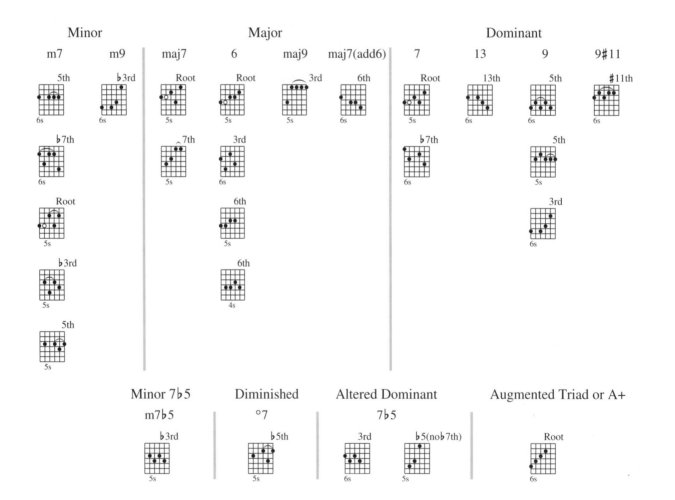

"Auld Lang Syne"–Chord Melody Arrangement

In this arrangement, we're NOT playing the melody an octave higher than it's written. Also, we're using two staves in an attempt to help you see what is going on here. The top staff is the melody and the lower staff is the chord melody arrangement.

Track 94

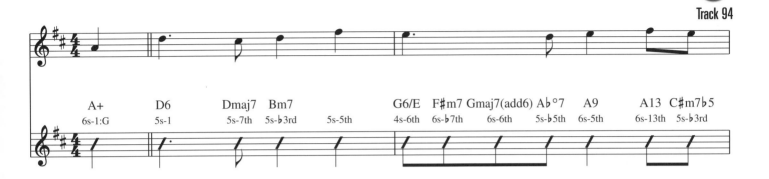

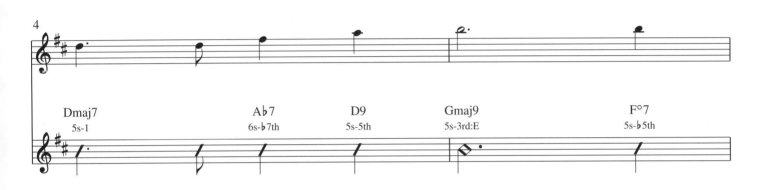

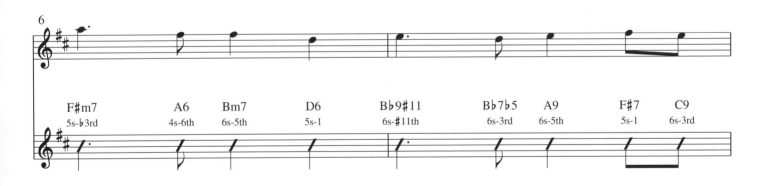

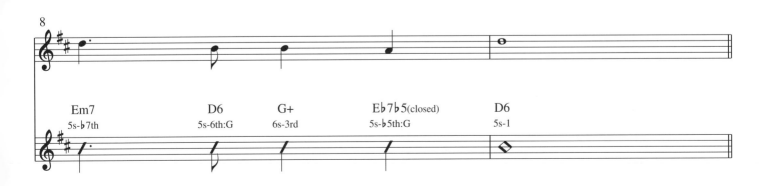

DANNY BOY

Given the 16-bar lead sheet to "Danny Boy" (below), let's transform it into a nice sounding chord melody arrangement.

Chord Voicings for This Exercise–Note: Root string is indicated below each diagram and highest chord tone is above each diagram.

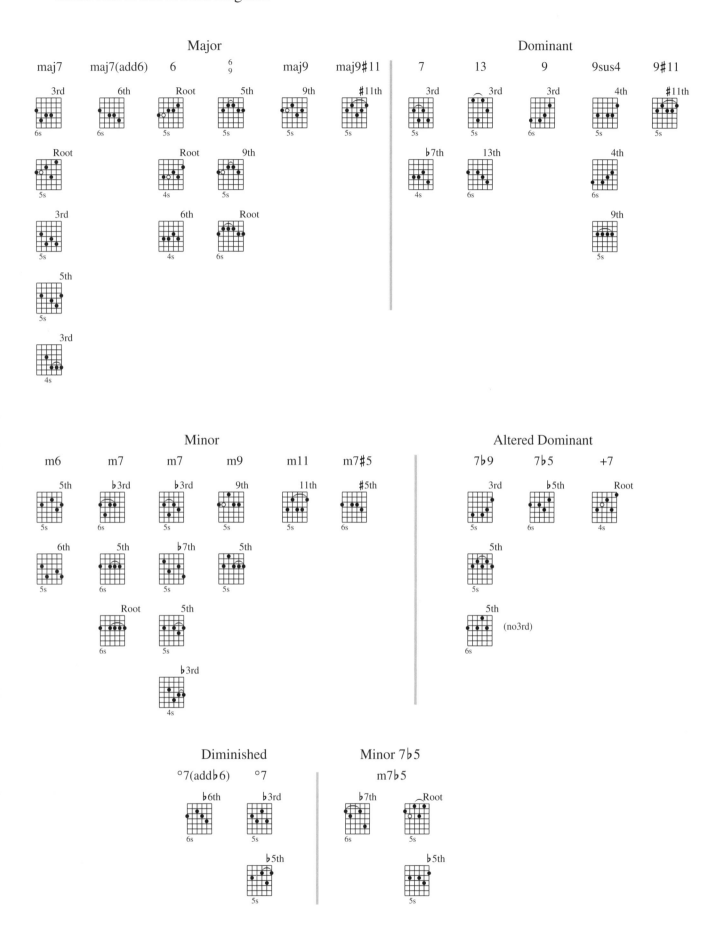

"Danny Boy"–Chord Melody Arrangement

In this arrangement, we are again playing the melody an octave higher than written.

Chord Soloing Section

Now we're going to look at some improvised chord solos. While chord soloing is a difficult skill to master, it is conceptually fairly simple. The basic idea is to look at the same scales used for improvising and then apply appropriate chords to each note in the scale. This is like chord melody playing except that we're improvising our own melodies.

So for a given chord progression like the one above...

First, decide on appropriate scales for the given chords. For each chord we can use a chord/scale from the exercises:

C Minor Scale using Chord Pair Approach—(Dorian Mode)

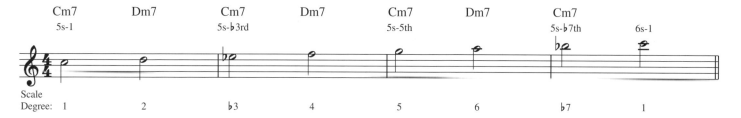

D minor 7♭5 Scale using Chord Pair Approach

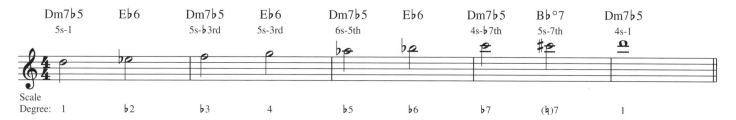

G Altered Dominant Scale using Chord Family Approach

Note: This scale example begins with C♯ in order to keep the top notes on the B and high E strings.

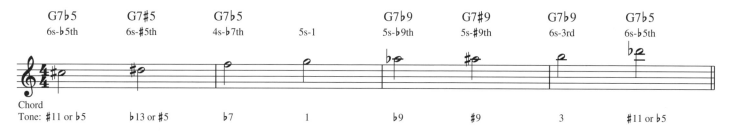

D♭ Major Scale using Chord Pair Approach

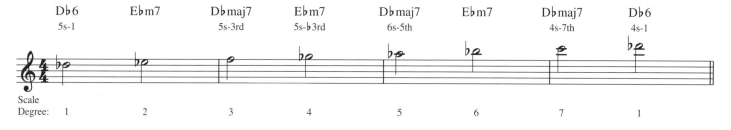

For the chord progression below, let's play a chord solo using the "Chord Pair Approach."

RISKY

Basic Chord Progression:

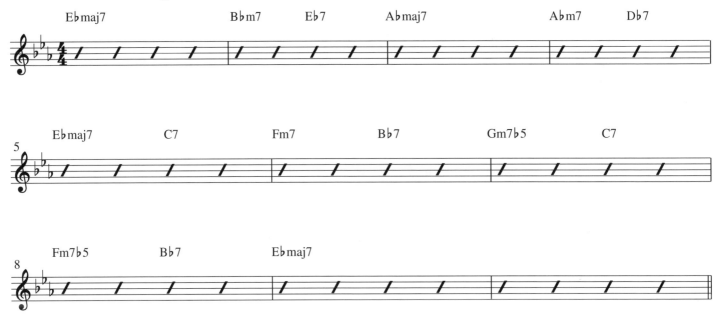

Chord Voicings for this Exercise

The chords from the scales used are shown below each chord change. Play these chords in sequence as indicated by the arrows before moving on to the actual chord solo. Note: Root string is indicated below each diagram and highest chord tone is above each diagram.

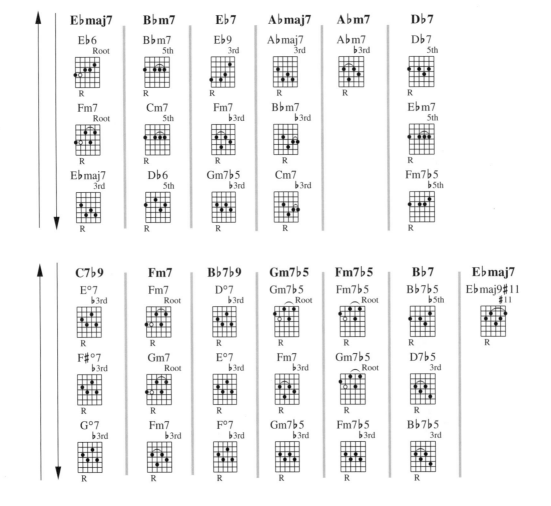

For this 10-bar study, we're using two staves in an attempt to help you see what is going on here. The top staff is the solo and the lower staff is the basic chord progression.

For the chord progression below, we're going to play a chord solo using the "Chord Pair Approach."

MY FUELISH CHART

Basic Chord Progression:

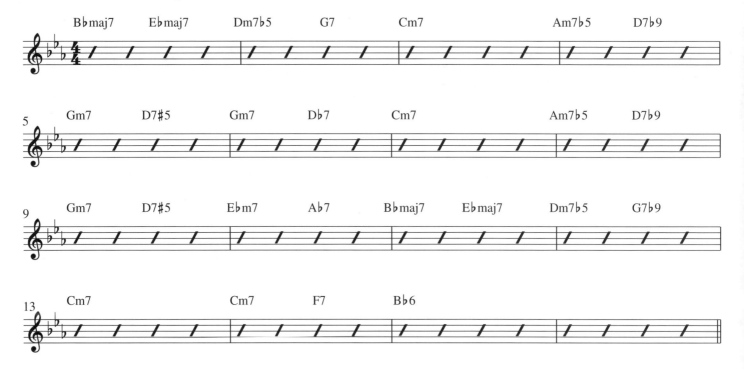

Chord Voicings for This Exercise

The chords from the scales that I used are shown below each chord change. Play these chords in sequence as indicated by the arrows before moving on to the actual chord solo. Note: Root string is indicated below each diagram and highest chord tone is above each diagram.

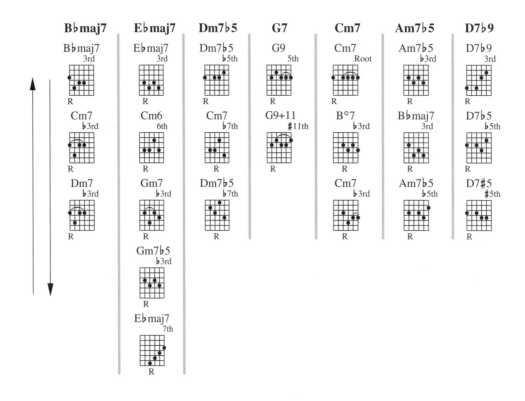

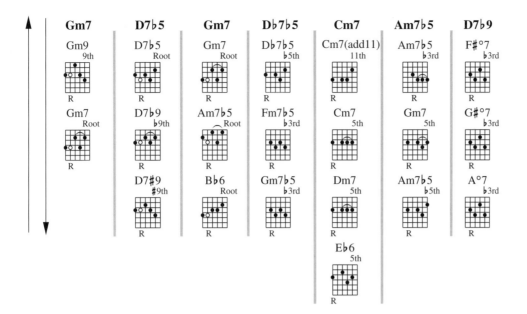

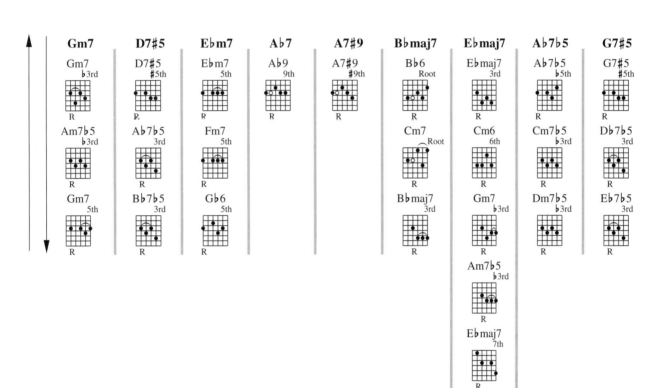

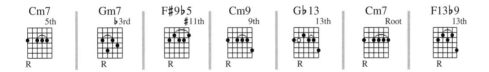

For this 20-bar study, we're using two staves in an attempt to help you see what is going on here.

Track 97

FALL TREES

For the chord progression below, let's play a chord solo using the "Alternating Chord/Note Style."

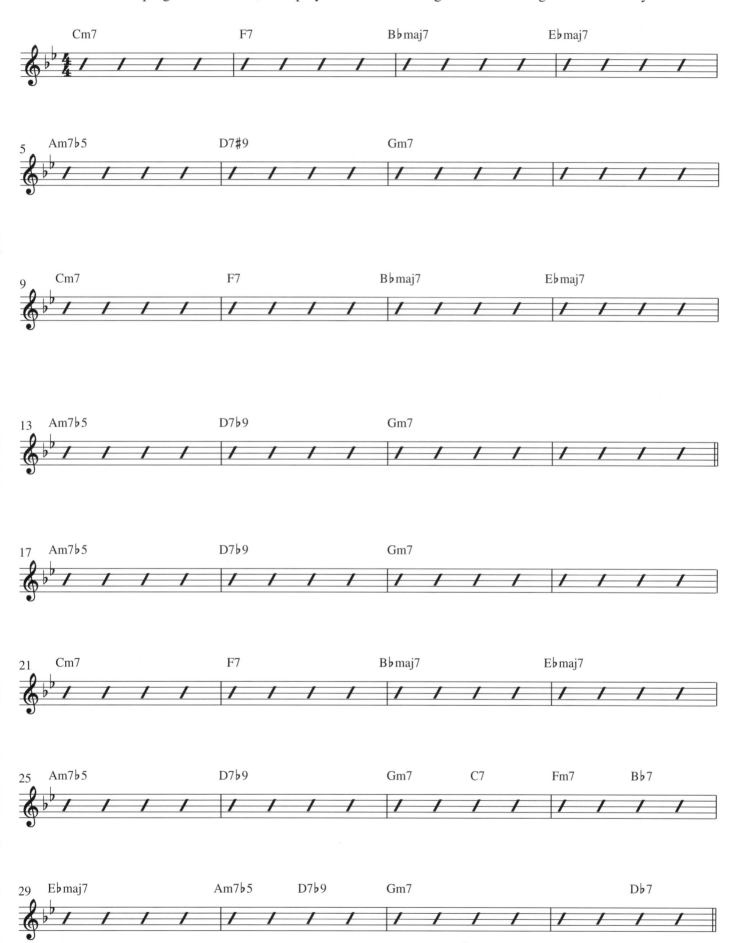

Chord Solo–Play appropriate chord on note indicated (↓) only.

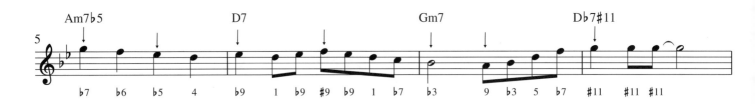

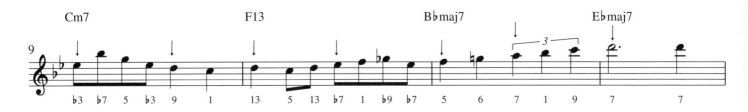

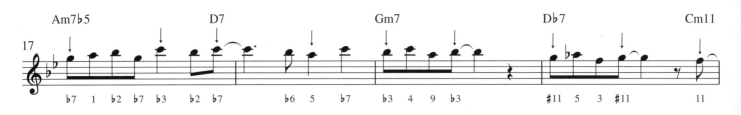

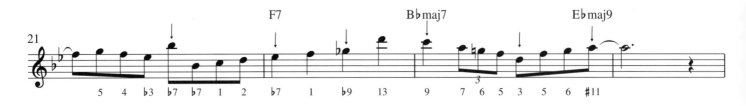

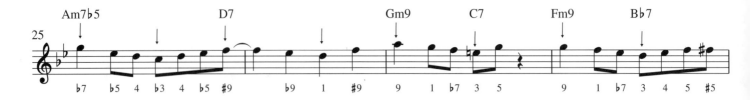

APPENDIX I:
Triads—Formula and Discussion

Triads are the basic building blocks of chords and as such we guitarists can benefit greatly from being able to recognize the triad structures in the voicings that we use. While a full triad study is beyond the scope of this book, please play and study the voicings and exercises in this section with the goal of gaining greater insight into the guitar fretboard as a whole.

MAJOR TRIAD SUMMARY

Major–closed

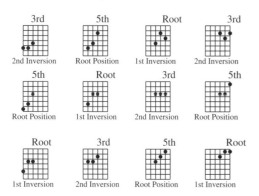

Major–open

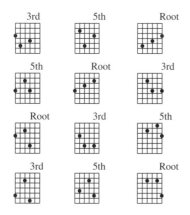

MINOR TRIAD SUMMARY

Minor–closed

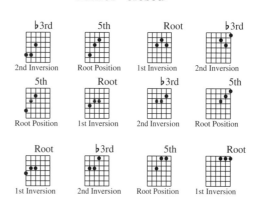

Minor–open

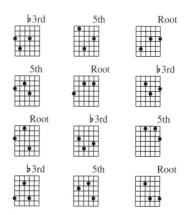

AUGMENTED TRIAD SUMMARY

Augmented–closed

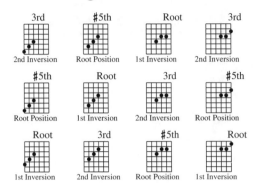

Augmented–open

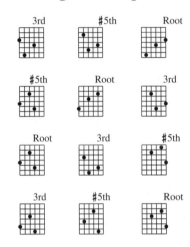

DIMINISHED TRIAD SUMMARY

Diminished–closed

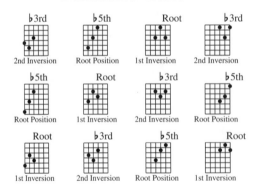

Diminished–open

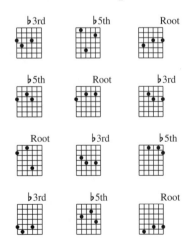

TRIAD SCALE EXERCISES

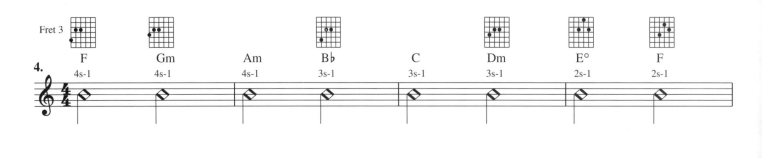

4.

Closed–
2nd Inv.

5.

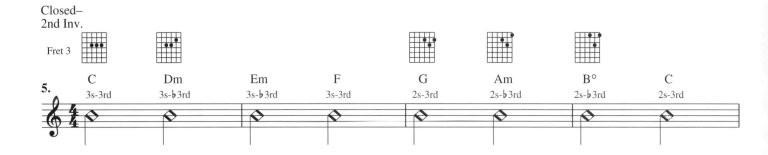

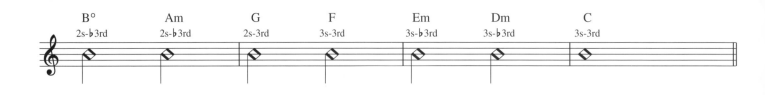

6.

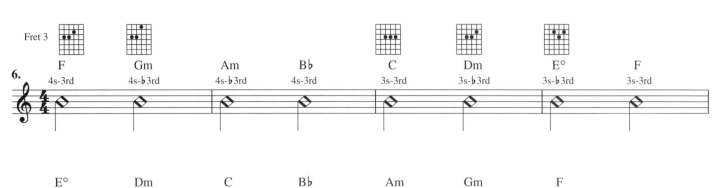

APPENDIX II:
Suggested Listening

Chords have played an integral role in the history of jazz guitar. While the guitar is not a horn or a piano, it has elements of both. It can even serve as a drum in the case of swing style rhythm guitar. Chords can transform a guitar into a miniature big band or orchestra.

Below is a list of artists and recordings for you to check out for some great chord work (and great playing in general!). Some of these recordings may be hard to find, so, in general, just try to get any recordings you find by these artists and study them intensely. Listen to the way they comp for themselves and others. Observe the way that they both solo and play melodies with chords. Please remember that this list is only a small sample of what is available. Try to expand your collection of recordings as much as you can and always take your listening very seriously.

Musician/Artist	Recording Title	Label, Catalog Number
Laurindo Almeida		
w/ Baden Powell	*Brasil Guitar Magic*	Fine Tune 2244
w/ Bud Shank	*Brazilliance Vol. 1*	Blue Note Records 96339
	Guitar From Ipanema	EMI TOCJ-6232
Gene Bertoncini		
w/ Michael Moore	*Two In Time*	Chiaroscuro 308
Ed Bickert		
w/ Paul Desmond	*The Paul Desmond Quartet Live*	Verve 543 501
Ed Bickert (Trio)	*Live With Fraser Macpherson*	DSM DSM2-3004
w/ Paul Desmond	*Pure Desmond*	CTI/CBS 40806
Lenny Breau		
	Live At Donte's	String Jazz 1008
	Five O'Clock Bells/Mo' Breau	Genes Records 5006/12
Kenny Burrell		
	Stolen Moments	Concord Jazz 2128
Charlie Byrd		
w/ Stan Getz	*Jazz Samba (+1 Bonus Track)*	POLY POCJ-9155
Oscar Castro-Neves		
Quartet...	*The Rhythm & The Sound Of Bossa Nova*	Ubatuqui 303
Freddie Green		
	Mr. Rhythm	Koch Jazz 8
		Giants Of Jazz Recordings (import) 53254

Jim Hall

w/ Paul Desmond	*The Paul Desmond Quartet With Jim Hall*	Giants Of Jazz Recordings (import) 53224
w/ Sonny Rollins	*Bridge*	05/02/2001
	Quartets FT Jim Hall	BMG ND85643

Rodney Jones

w/ T. Flanagan	*My Funny Valentine*	07/15/1993

Barney Kessel

w/ Shelly Manne, Ray Brown

	Poll Winners Three! [Remaster]	Contemporary Records 7535
	Autumn Leaves [Remaster]	1201 Music 9018

Earl Klugh

	Volume 1 Earl Klugh Trio	Warner Bros. Records 26750
	Solo Guitar	Warner Bros.

Russell Malone

Diana Krall	*All for You*	Impulse! 182
Diana Krall	*Love Scenes*	GRP Records 233

Pat Martino

	El Hombre	Original Jazz Classics 195

Pat Metheny

Joshua Redman	*Wish*	Warner Bros. Records 45365

Wes Montgomery

	Full House	Original Jazz Classics 106
w/ Joe Williams	*At Jorgie's 1961 & 1963*	09/18/2001
Wes Montgomery Trio	*Wes Montgomery Trio*	Original Jazz Classics 034
w/ Wynton Kelly Trio	*Smokin' at the Half Note*	Verve 829 578

Joe Pass

w/ Ella Fitzgerald	*Take Love Easy (Remastered)*	PABLO VICJ-60319
w/ Toots Thielemans	*Live in Netherlands*	STAX 188048
	Virtuoso [Remaster]	Pablo Records 2310-708
w/ Herb Ellis, Ray Brown	*Arrival*	01/28/2003
w/ Ella Fitzgerald	*Speak Love (JPN)(Limited Edition)*	01/02/2002
w/ Ella Fitzgerald	*Fitzgerald & Pass...Again*	11/20/2001
w/ Ella Fitzgerald	*Nice Work if You Can Get It...*	11/20/2001
w/ J.J. Johnson	*We'll Be Together Again*	Pablo Records 909

Bucky Pizzarelli

w/ Scott Hamilton	*The Red Door...Remember Zoot Sims*	Concord Jazz 4799
	Solos & Duets	Jazz Classics 5007

Johnny Smith

	The Sound of the Johnny Smith Guitar	Roulette Records 31792
Johnny Smith Quintet	*Moonlight in Vermont*	Blue Note Records 97747
	New Quartet	

Martin Taylor

| | *In Concert* | Milestone Records 9306 |

George Van Eps

| | *Soliloquy* | Sundazed Music Inc. 193 |

Piano Players

Additionally, it is important to listen to piano players for more insight into various ways of applying chords in jazz. Here is a partial list of piano players to study:

Barry Harris, Bill Evans, Cedar Walton, Chick Corea, Keith Jarrett, George Shearing, Hank Jones, Herbie Hancock, Oscar Peterson, Red Garland, Tommy Flanagan, Wynton Kelly, Jimmy Smith (organ), McCoy Tyner.

Big Bands

Big band music can also be a good source of chord ideas. Listen to the intros, endings, etc. Also listen to the harmonies in the various sections. Equally important, but often overlooked, are the rhythms used in the ensembles. Some big bands to check out include:

Count Basie Orchestra, Duke Ellington Orchestra, Stan Kenton Orchestra, Woody Herman Big Band.

Final Thoughts

What's Next? Beyond Basic Chords

I certainly hope that you will continue to grow as a musician and person. While this book addresses some basic chord structures and concepts, the continued study of chords and harmony can go on forever! Below are some other areas for you to explore:

1. Drop-note chords and rootless voicings
2. Modal harmony
3. Quartal harmony
4. Other scales harmonized
5. Polychords w/guide tone under structure
6. Walking bass lines with chords
7. Self-accompaniment
8. Learning as many tunes as possible (especially jazz standards)

Also, it is important to play with other musicians. Try to learn something from every musician that you play with, and play as often as possible. Purchase a small cassette or mini disc recorder and record yourself as often as possible. Hearing yourself from an external perspective will be of great benefit to you. It has been my experience in studying music and the guitar that drawing on as many sources as possible for information leads to the best results. In other words, find good teachers, books, magazines, videos, CDs, internet sources, etc. for information. Exposure is everything!

IMPROVE YOUR IMPROV
AND OTHER JAZZ TECHNIQUES WITH BOOKS FROM HAL LEONARD

JAZZ GUITAR
THE COMPLETE GUIDE
HAL LEONARD GUITAR METHOD
by Jeff Schroedl
The Hal Leonard Jazz Guitar Method is your complete guide to learning jazz guitar. This book uses real jazz songs to teach you the basics of accompanying and improvising jazz guitar in the style of Wes Montgomery, Joe Pass, Tal Farlow, Charlie Christian, Pat Martino, Barney Kessel, Jim Hall, and many others.
_____00695359 Book/CD Pack.........................$12.95

BEST OF JAZZ GUITAR
by Wolf Marshall • Signature Licks
Explore the music of the world's greatest jazz guitarists! In this book/CD pack, Wolf Marshall provides a hands-on analysis of 10 of the most frequently played tunes in the jazz genre, as played by the leading guitarists of all time. Features: "St. Thomas" performed by Jim Hall, Tal Farlow and Kenny Burrell • "All Blues" performed by George Benson, Kenny Burrell and Pat Martino • "Satin Doll" performed by Howard Roberts and Joe Pass • "I'll Remember April" performed by Johnny Smith and Grant Green • and more! Each selection includes technical analysis and performance notes, biographical sketches, and authentic matching audio with backing tracks.
"This is a wonderful undertaking – a good selection of music well-played. To hear and study all the jazz guitar greats of yesterday and today like this will be of immense value to all players." – Herb Ellis
_____00695586 Book/CD Pack.........................$24.95

CHORD-MELODY PHRASES FOR GUITAR
by Ron Eschete
REH • ProLessons Series
Expand your chord-melody chops with these outstanding jazz phrases by Ron Eschete! He covers: chord substitutions, chromatic movements, contrary motion, pedal tones, inner-voice movements, reharmonization techniques, and much more. The book includes standard notation and tablature, and the CD features 39 helpful demo tracks.
_____00695628 Book/CD Pack.........................$14.95

JAZZ IMPROVISATION FOR GUITAR
by Les Wise • REH • ProLessons Series
This terrific book/CD by Les Wise will allow you to make the transition from playing disjointed scales and arpeggios to playing melodic jazz solos that maintain continuity and interest for the listener. Topics covered include: tension and resolution • major scale, melodic minor scale, and harmonic minor scale patterns • common licks and substitution techniques • creating altered tension • and more! Features standard notation and tab, and a CD with 35 demo tracks.
_____00695657 Book/CD Pack.........................$16.95

JAZZ RHYTHM GUITAR
THE COMPLETE GUIDE
by Jack Grassel
This book/CD pack by award-winning guitarist and distinguished teacher Jack Grassel will help rhythm guitarists better understand: chord symbols and voicings; comping styles and patterns; equipment, accessories and set-up; the fingerboard; chord theory; and much more. The accompanying CD includes 74 full-band tracks.
_____00695654 Book/CD Pack.........................$19.95

JAZZ SOLOS FOR GUITAR
Lead guitar in the Styles of Tal Farlow,
Barney Kessel, Wes Montgomery, Joe Pass, Johnny Smith
by Les Wise
Examine the solo concepts of the masters in this unique book/CD package. The CD includes full demonstration and rhythm-only tracks to assist with learning the styles of Kenny Burrell, Jim Hall, Barney Kessel, Pat Martino, Wes Montgomery, Joe Pass, Johnny Smith, and others. The book includes phrase-by-phrase performance notes, tips on arpeggio substitution, scale substitution, tension and resolution, jazz-blues, chord soloing, and much more.
_____00695447 Book/CD Pack.........................$17.95

THE MOTIVIC BASIS FOR JAZZ GUITAR IMPROVISATION
by Steve Rochinski
A method for creating jazz lines in the style of Charlie Parker, Charlie Christian, Tal Farlow, Jimmy Raney, and others. The CD includes performance examples and backing tracks from an all-star rhythm section. Book includes dozens of essential licks and phrases in standard notation and easy-to-read guitar neck diagrams.
_____00695257 Book/CD Pack.........................$14.95

101 MUST-KNOW JAZZ LICKS
A Quick, Easy Reference for All Guitarists
by Wolf Marshall
Now you can add authentic jazz feel and flavor to your playing! Here are 101 definitive licks, plus a demonstration CD, from every major jazz guitar style, neatly organized into easy-to-use categories. They're all here: swing and pre-bop, bebop, post-bop modern jazz, hard bop and cool jazz, modal jazz, soul jazz and postmodern jazz. Includes an introduction by Wolf Marshall, tips for using the book and CD, and a listing of suggested recordings.
_____00695433 Book/CD Pack.........................$16.95

SWING AND BIG BAND GUITAR
FOUR-TO-THE-BAR COMPING IN
THE STYLE OF FREDDIE GREEN
by Charlton Johnson
This unique package teaches the essentials of swing and big band styles, including chord voicings, inversions, substitutions; time and groove, reading charts, chord reduction, and expansion; sample songs, patterns, progressions, and exercises; chord reference library; and a CD with over 50 full-demo examples. Uses chord grids – no tablature.
_____00695147 Book/CD Pack...................$16.95

Prices, contents and availability subject to change without notice.